Songs of a

THE MARY O'LEARY STORY

Brian Brennan

First published as Máire Bhuí Ní Laoire: A Poet of her People, by
The Collins Press, Cork, Ireland, 2000.
ISBN 1-898256-98-5

To Kieran

CONTENTS

About the Author

Brian Brennan is an Irish-born author and journalist who immigrated to Canada in 1966. He lives and writes in Calgary, Alberta, and specializes in books about the colourful personalities and the social history of Western Canada. His maternal grandmother, Hannah Twomey (née Burke), was the great-granddaughter of Mary O'Leary.

Acknowledgments

This book is based on several published and anecdotal sources, the principal reference being *Filíocht Mháire Bhuidhe ní Laoghaire* (literally, The Poetry of Yellow Mary O'Leary) by An tAthair Donncha Ó Donnchú (Fr. Denis O'Donoghue) MA, who served as assistant parish priest in the West Cork parish of Ballingeary in 1917. His 95-page, red-backed book of Mary O'Leary's songs was originally published in 1931 by the Irish government printing office but it has been out of print since the 1950s. It was felicitously translated for me, in stages, by Hugh O'Donnell, Kieran J. Desmond, Michael Desmond, and Larry McCurry. Having used their translations to complete the first part of this manuscript, I was introduced to a further translation of *Filíocht Mháire Bhuidhe ní Laoghaire* which proved to be a most valuable resource. It was privately published in 1996 by two priests, Fr. Richard P. Burke SJ of College of the Holy Cross, Worcester, Massachusetts, and Father Seán Sweeney SMA of Dedham, Massachusetts. They produced it as a non-profit venture for circulation to about 150 people, and their labour of love immensely aided mine. All the mysteries of the little red-backed book were finally unlocked for me. I wrote to Fr. Burke in July 1999, to tell him how much I appreciated his work only to discover, sadly, that he had died two months earlier. I would like to believe he would have given his blessing to this work.

Other texts consulted include *Family Names of County Cork* by Diarmuid O'Murchadha (Glendale Press 1985, The Collins Press 1996), and *Cork History & Society: Interdisciplinary Essays on the History of an Irish County*, edited by Patrick O'Flanagan and Cornelius G. Buttimer (Geography Publications, 1993). Additional historical material was drawn from *An Illustrated History of the Irish People* by Kenneth Neill (Mayflower Books, 1979). West Cork genealogist Mary Casey provided anecdotal material. While others have provided the raw material for this manuscript, I take full responsibility for whatever interpretation or emphasis I may have placed on the facts supplied.

I would like to pay tribute to Helen Davis, the Special Collections Librarian at University College Cork, who was most helpful to me, as were several of her colleagues including Seán Ua Suilleabháin, who translated some reference material for me. An additional salute goes to the gas pump attendant in Inchigeelagh, County Cork, who pointed me in the direction of Mary O'Leary's gravesite. Other valuable help in Inchigeelagh came from Seán O'Sullivan of the Ballingeary Historical Society who has worked hard to preserve the memory of Mary O'Leary. In 1998, members of the Ballingeary Society joined forces with the Bantry Historical Society to erect a monument in the Pass of Keimaneigh commemorating the 1822 battle that is the subject of Mary O'Leary's best-known poem.

Special personal thanks goes to my daughter, Nicole Brennan, who returned from a year-long stay in Ireland with a wonderful gift: a rare hardback copy of *Filíocht Mháire Bhuidhe ní Laoghaire*, the little red-covered book that inspired me to write this book. The love and support of my wife Zelda sustained me through the tougher parts of the research and the writing, when my failing memory of the Irish language, and my struggles to reconcile conflicting historical data, conspired to sink this project.

My greatest debt is to the dedicatee of this book, my first cousin and fellow Mary O'Leary descendant Kieran Desmond, who provided unfailing support and enthusiasm for this labour of love. He assisted me substantially at every stage of the work, and gave me many useful comments on the finished manuscript.

Brian Brennan, September 2007

Author's note

In Irish writings, the Gaelic version of the name O'Leary is variously spelt Ó'Laoghaire or O'Laoire. I have chosen the newer Irish spelling, O'Laoire (or Ní Laoire in its feminine form), for the most part, while alternating that with the English version, O'Leary, whenever it serves to separate a person of one generation from a similarly-named member of another generation. The O'Leary clan, throughout the centuries, used such a limited range of first names that confusion inevitably arises. I have done the same for other Gaelic proper names throughout the manuscript, trying to maintain some consistency in the simplification and spelling of the names, particularly place names. But there may be some lapses. Maps and authors do not always agree. Neither do writers in Irish, who substitute the letter "i" for the letter "a", or the letter "e" for the letter "a", seemingly at will.

The following is a partial list of some first names used in the text, and their equivalents in English:

IRISH NAME	ENGLISH VERSION
Brighid, Bríd	Brigid, Bridget
Cáit	Kate, Kathleen
Crochúr, Conchobhar	Con(n)or, Cornelius
Diarmuid, Diarmaid	Dermot, Jeremiah
Domhnall, Dónal	Donal, Donald
Donnchadh	Den(n)is
Eibhlín	Eileen, Ellen
Eilic	Alec, Alex, Alexander
Maighréad	Margaret
Máire	Mary, Maura
Micheál	Michael
Neil (f)	Nell, Ellen
Neil (m)	Neil, Cornelius
Nóra	Nora, Honorah, Honna
Pádraig	Patrick
Risteárd	Richard
Séamas, Séamus	James

Seán	John
Síle	Sheila, Julia
Siobhán	Joan, Johanna, Hannah,
Tadhg	Timothy, Teigue

INTRODUCTION

Máire Bhuí Ní Laoire (literally, Yellow Mary O'Leary) was a true local heroine, a popular Munster folk poet of the nineteenth century whose creative contribution barely registers a blip on the radar screens of Irish literary scholarship.

While she does rate a one-paragraph mention in Robert Welch's authoritative *The Oxford Companion To Irish Literature* (Clarendon, 1996), she does not appear at all in such English-language surveys of Irish literature as the magisterial *An Duanaire, (Poetry Anthology) 1600-1900: Poems Of The Dispossessed* by Seán Ó Tuama and Thomas Kinsella (Dolmen Press, 1981).

One reason for this may be that Mary O'Leary came from an Irish literary tradition that remains virtually inaccessible to all but the Irish-speaking or Irish-reading minority of the Irish people.

Another likely reason for her obscurity is that Mary O'Leary composed her verses to be sung and never wrote them down. They were passed down orally from generation to generation. This puts her on the far side of the class divide separating the less privileged strata of Irish society — characterized by oral tradition, the Irish language and poverty — from the side representing literacy, English, and all the trappings of patriarchal and colonialist modernity.

The oral tradition, as the critic Angela Bourke has noted in her essay, "Performing not Writing: The Reception of an Irish Woman's Lament,"[1] needs no endorsement from the world of written literature to ensure its validity or survival.

But the world of writing persists in speaking of and for it, and it is in the spirit of what Ó Tuama and Kinsella might call "repossession"[2] that I have written this book about the life and oral poetry of Mary O'Leary.

Oral poems are often presented in literary anthologies as the work of "Anonymous" who, as Virginia Woolf wryly remarked, was probably a woman. However, happily for Irish literary historians,

---

[1] *Dwelling in Possibility: Women Poets and Critics on Poetry,* edited by Yopie Prins and Maeera Shreiber (Cornell University Press, 1997)
[2] *An Duanaire 1600-1900: Poems of the Dispossessed* by Seán Ó Tuama and Thomas Kinsella (Dolmen Press, 1981)

11

Mary O'Leary was not one such anonymous female. Her works were eventually collected, written down, and preserved. They survive not only in the folklore of West Cork but also in the archives of such institutions as University College Cork and the Ballingeary Historical Society of West Cork. Additionally, they survive in the curricula of the Irish-speaking schools of Munster, and in such Irish-language anthologies as *Filíocht na nGael* (Poetry of the Irish) by Padraig Ó'Canainn (An Press Náisiúnta, 1958), though many of these collections are now out of print.

Born in 1774 near Inchigeelagh, Co. Cork, into the *Buí* (Yellow) branch of the O'Leary clan which once held the local lands under the patronage of the higher-ranking MacCarthy overlords, Mary O'Leary composed poetry of a kind that demands a listening rather than a reading audience. This poses a challenge for a modern outsider endeavouring to assess her artistic contribution. While a spirited and lyrically appropriate translation of her works might serve to give some sense of her literary achievement, there is no way of knowing what kind of artistry she might have brought to the oral performance. One encounters a similar problem when trying to evaluate the artistic merit of rock music lyrics existing in isolation from the music and the performance.

One can never fully appreciate, for example, the power of the laments that Mary O'Leary composed in response to local tragic events. Lamenting the dead was a central component of funeral ritual in Ireland until modern times. The woman who led the "keening" (lamenting) was both poet and performer. She assumed ownership of the community's grief and expressed it in all its complexity with her words, appearance, behaviour and voice.

Mary O'Leary composed several laments. She also composed love songs, religious meditations and humorous pieces reflecting the life of her community. Sometimes, she ventured beyond the limits of the oral folk genre into the realm of higher literary tradition recalling the distant poetic masters of the 17th and eighteenth centuries. Her use of the *aisling* or vision-poem form, for example, hearkens back to a style favoured by Egan O'Rahilly (1670-1726) and Owen Roe O'Sullivan (1748-84). In her poem *Ar Leacain na Gréine* ("On a Sunny Hillside") she encounters a fairy woman of outstanding beauty who foretells the defeat of the English despite the failure of the French general Lazare Hoche's invasion of 1796.

Perhaps Mary O'Leary's best-known poem is *Cath Chéim an Fhia* ("The Battle of Keimaneigh") which gives a lively, if somewhat exaggerated account of an 1822 clash between a secret society of tenant farmers known as the Whiteboys or the Rockites, and the local battalion of yeomanry — a volunteer cavalry force raised from the landlord class by Lord Bantry. Mary O'Leary was a witness to some of the battle, which involved several members of her family and took place not far from her home.

The creators of poetry anthologies, and others who confer the approval of the English literary tradition on Irish oral poetry, have paid scant attention to the creative output of Mary O'Leary. This is a shame because Mary O'Leary emerges as one of the very few female Irish-language poets to achieve name recognition during the period from medieval times to the present. The only other female Gaelic poet to achieve similar recognition was Eibhlín Dhubh Ní Chomhnaill (Dark-haired Eileen O'Connell) whose sole remembered contribution is the poem *Caoine Airt Uí Laoghaire* ("Lament for Art O'Leary"), an eighteenth century masterpiece in the lyric "keening" tradition.[3]

Mary O'Leary left her mark during the nineteenth century when the government policies initiated in Tudor times for eliminating the Irish language finally began to bear fruit. By the end of the century, the English language was the common currency of the Irish people. During the last part of this long, three-century gap between the collapse of the old Gaelic tradition of artistic patronage for hereditary bardic poets, and the emergence of English as the dominant vernacular of the Irish people, Mary O'Leary stood tall as the standard-bearer for those communities who used verse instinctively as a vehicle for recording the events of everyday life.

Though they did not mention her specifically by name, I like to believe that Ó Tuama and Kinsella might have had Mary O'Leary in mind when they declared, in their introduction to *An Duanaire*, that Gaelic verse in the nineteenth century, though of minor artistic interest, had "more vitality on the whole, and more reference to life as lived, than the bulk of nineteenth century Irish verse written in English."

---

[3] See Appendix A.

THE O'LEARY CLAN

Cois abhainn Ghleanna an Chéama
in Uíbh Laoire 'sea bhímse.

Near the river bank in Keimaneigh
in Iveleary I spend my time.

So sang Mary O'Leary, the poet of her clan, in the opening lines of her most famous poem, composed to commemorate the Battle of Keimaneigh in 1822. Her choice of the ancient place name *Uíbh Laoghaire* (literally: descendants of Laoghaire) is significant. For Mary O'Leary, as for many of her clan, *Uíbh Laoghaire* (or in its English dress, Iveleary) meant the sprawling parish of Inchigeelagh, West Cork, a region that served for centuries as the habitat of the O'Learys, one of the most tightly knit and deeply rooted of the old Gaelic septs or clans.

The O'Learys settled in Inchigeelagh after they were expelled from their ancestral homeland circa 1192. They came initially from the rocky seacoast of southwest County Cork, the peninsular region southwest of Clonakilty between Rosscarbery and Glandore. Their forebears were members of an ancient Munster tribe known as *Corca Laoí* (the People of the River Lee).

The O'Learys were banished from the Rosscarbery area by two other Gaelic septs, named O'Donovan and O'Collins, who had themselves been driven by Anglo-Norman invaders from their lands in County Limerick. The O'Learys did not flee far, however. They migrated just a few miles northward to the remote mountain region of Inchigeelagh. [4]

Here, in the lea of the overshadowing Kerry Mountains, the O'Learys ruled under the protection of the higher-ranking MacCarthys who, as Gaelic overlords of the barony of Muskerry, politically dominated the entire western half of County Cork. The

---

[4] *Gaelic Land Tenure in County Cork: Uíbh Laoghaire in the Seventeenth Century*, by Diarmuid O'Murchadha. This essay appears as Chapter 7, pp. 213-48, of the anthology *Cork History & Society: Interdisciplinary Essays on the History of an Irish County*, editors Patrick O'Flanagan, Cornelius G. Buttimer (Geography Publications, 1993).

Muskerry MacCarthys were, in turn, a branch of the MacCarthy *Mór* (Large) dynasty of Desmond, which ruled the southern half of the province of Munster (*Deas + Mhumhan* = south Munster) from the twelfth to the sixteenth century.

The O'Learys in Inchigeelagh remained virtually unaffected by the MacCarthy hegemony, especially after the MacCarthys gained control of Muskerry in the fourteenth century. With the MacCarthys thus preoccupied, the O'Learys maintained a high degree of independence, which lasted until the seventeenth century.

CELTIC TRADITION REMAINED STRONG

Though ranked as Cork's third-largest civil and ecclesiastical parish, with its 118 townlands (45,415 statute acres), Inchigeelagh before the late sixteenth century qualified as little more than an insignificant lordship in an upland district. It was not considered worthy of mention, either in official English documents or in Irish annals or bardic poetry. This remoteness from extraneous influences contributed to the preservation of a unique system of land division, dating back to pre-Christian Celtic times.

Paternal ancestry dictated the way in which land passed from one generation of O'Learys to the next. The inheritance system was complicated, however, by the fact that first-born succession was not customary. Like the Celts, the O'Learys did not practise primogeniture. Their first-born received no preference in matters of inheritance or succession. An O'Leary clan chief could be succeeded by any of his male relatives who shared the same great-grandfather. This rather large group would include his brothers, nephews, first and second cousins, as well as members of his immediate family. A review of the O'Leary genealogy shows many instances where property passed from grandfather to grandson, from uncle to nephew, cousin to cousin, and so on. This system prevailed until the early seventeenth century, when the old Celtic laws, under which the Irish had lived for more than a thousand years, were finally repealed.

The O'Learys were land-holding cattlemen, occupying townlands given to them by their MacCarthy overlords, one of whom lived nearby. This arrangement, too, derived from Celtic tradition. The only Irish settlements faintly resembling towns in Celtic Ireland were the clustered dwellings of peasant kinsmen gathered around the larger homes of local kings or important nobles. It was these clusters or "towns" that gave the Irish "townland" — a small territorial subdivision averaging about half a square mile in area — its English name.

The O'Learys were the spiritual descendants of a land-holding farming class that was the foundation of Celtic society. The yeoman farmer of this period was known as a *bóaire*, literally a cattleman. Wealth was measured in cattle, not in land. A nobleman rented out his cattle with the understanding that the *bóaire* — in addition to repaying the lord in milk and calves — would also provide certain personal and military services. Living off leases of great herds of cattle, the Celtic nobility was thus an idle class that could afford to devote its energies to warfare, the time-honoured sport of aristocrats. Combat invariably revolved around cattle raids, as groups of noblemen tried to increase their supply of this most valuable resource.

Over time, land gradually replaced cattle as the basic economic unit of agricultural value. Because the ability of a *bóaire* to build up his herd depended on appropriating sufficient grazing lands, an agriculture system based solely upon the leasing of cattle eventually made no sense. By the eighth century, Celtic nobles found it more useful to make tenancy arrangements with their clients rather than rent them cattle. Wars between neighbouring chieftains thus evolved from cattle raids into territorial clashes.[5]

THE NORMANS MOVE WESTWARD

According to one published report, the O'Learys occupied townlands between Rosscarbery and Glandore in Southwest County Cork until after the Anglo-Norman conquest began in 1169.[6]

Some twenty years earlier, the English-born Pope Hadrian IV had granted Henry II, the Norman king of England, the title "Lord of Ireland," hoping this might encourage the king to help reorganize the Irish church. In the process, the Pope established a quasi-legal basis for English conquest and occupation of Ireland. The Anglo-Norman invasion of Ireland did not, however, destroy the sovereignty of the

---

[5] *An Illustrated History of the Irish People*, by Kenneth Neill (Mayflower Books, 1979) pp. 15-22).

[6] *Parish of Inchigeelagh* by John Lyons PP. in the Journal of the Cork Historical and Archaeological Society, Vol. II, pp. 77-78.

old Gaelic kingdoms. It merely imposed the authority of the English king on a few Irish coastal towns and their immediate territories.

The original Norman invaders of England — sophisticated European warriors of Viking ancestry, with special talents for warfare and efficient government — had been given free settlement of Wales and were spoiling for Ireland. Their opportunity came when Diarmuid MacMurrough, the deposed ruler of Leinster — one of five large kingdoms in Celtic Ireland — turned to King Henry II for help. Henry granted permission for an army to be raised from the Welsh Normans. With them as allies, Diarmuid quickly regained his Leinster kingdom. He might also have gained the high kingship of the entire country, but his death prevented it. He died suddenly in 1177, two years after the Norman soldiers arrived. The Welsh-Norman warrior knight Richard de Clare, earl of Pembroke — better known by his evocative nickname, Strongbow — succeeded Diarmuid. This was because Diarmuid had made Strongbow a most tempting offer to guarantee his support: the hand of his daughter in marriage, and with it the opportunity to inherit the kingship of Leinster.

The Gaelic chieftains, who had long engaged in unsophisticated tribal warfare, were no match for these well-equipped Norman warriors. They capitulated in short order. By the year 1200, a handful of Norman lords controlled three-quarters of Ireland. It was only a token victory, however. King Henry II had entered into treaty obligations with the Irish kings, acknowledging the validity of their royal houses.

Thus, the Norman Conquest of Ireland, as historian Magnus Magnusson says, was only half a conquest. While Norman barons controlled much of the country, and developed new patterns of trade, they never succeed in doing what they had done in England, i.e. creating a new nation combining the characteristics of natives and invaders alike.[7]

THE O'LEARYS SETTLE IN INCHIGEELAGH

The O'Learys migrated northward from their ancestral homelands in southwest County Cork, eventually settling under the patronage of the MacCarthys — who retained their feudal territories in the face of the Norman invasion — in the area adjoining the River Lee, between

---

[7] *Landlord or Tenant?* by Magnus Magnusson (Bodley Head, 1978), p. 13.

Inchigeelagh and Gougane Barra. This remote mountain district, roughly bounded by Toon Bridge, Keimaneigh, the Shehy Mountains and Toon River, became known as the O'Leary territory, then Iveleary now Inchigeelagh.

Despite its remoteness, Iveleary was far from being a no-man's land before the O'Learys arrived. The abundance of such Celtic archeological sites as wedge-tombs, standing stones, ring-forts (homestead sites), stone and wooden dwellings attests to a continuity of occupation for many centuries before the coming of the Normans. As part of the kingdom of Desmond, Iveleary may also have provided secure refuge for MacCarthy leaders pursued by Anglo-Norman antagonists.

When the MacCarthys asserted their dominance in the barony of Muskerry during the fourteenth century, they granted thirty of their townlands to the O'Leary clan. The O'Learys initially occupied the Inchigeelagh territory as freeholders, and eventually paid a nominal rent of twenty-four cattle plus £7 2s. 3d annually.

As part of the rental deal, the O'Learys were obliged to give the MacCarthy *tánaiste* (crown prince) two days and nights of free room and board, once every quarter. Additionally, the *tánaiste*, who lived in a castle at Carrignamuck, south of Ballingeary, qualified for a payment of £4 9s. every time a new O'Leary chief was elected. A further condition was that the O'Learys would assist the MacCarthys whenever they engaged in territorial wars with their neighbours. The fortunes of the O'Learys were thus inextricably linked to how well the MacCarthys fared in battle. Marriages between O'Learys and MacCarthys also served to link the two clans.

THREE CASTLES BUILT

During the 1500s, the O'Learys constructed three stone tower-houses or small castles as fortifications in the region. They built the main one near Carrignaneelagh (Rock of the Captives), three miles east of the present township of Inchigeelagh. This edifice no longer exists. On the Ordnance Survey of Ireland map (Discovery Series 86), its site is marked near Kilbarry Hill. It was built around 1565 and occupied by clan chief Art O'Laoire during Elizabethan times — when the first records of the O'Learys began to appear in such documents as the *O'Clery Book of Genealogies* and Eothan Ó Caoimh's *An Leabhar Mhuimhneach* (The Book of Munster). Art's genealogy can be traced back through about twenty-five generations to the original Laoghaire whose name, in Irish, means "keeper of calves."

Art's grandfather Diarmuid (Dermot or Jeremiah) O'Laoire, who lived in the early sixteenth century, is the first to be named in the O'Leary genealogies as duly elected lord or chief of the clan. The election would have taken place, according to Gaelic-Celtic tradition, with votes cast by men whose fathers, grandfathers, or great-grandfathers had been chiefs.

Art's father Conchobhar (Cornelius or Conor), who died about 1576, is the first chief about whom detailed information is available. A 1626 government survey found that he had held extensive townlands north of the River Lee, including such properties as Glasheen, Cloonshear Beg, Milleen, and Derryvane.

Both Art and his father were involved, albeit indirectly, with the first Desmond rebellion of the 1570s, when the hereditary Old English (Anglo-Norman) earl of southern Munster, Gerald FitzThomas, tried unsuccessfully to "defend our Catholic faith against Englishmen which have overrun our country."[8]

Art and his father Conchobhar (identified in official English documents as "Cnogher M'Dermode O Leary of Inshygyelaghe") were pardoned in 1573 for their role in the Desmond rebellion.[9] Subsequent pardons were issued to Art in 1584, 1585, and 1587, although these pardons seem to have been more in the nature of indemnities than actual absolution for rebellious deeds allegedly perpetrated by Art. As chief representative of the clan, Art would not — openly at any rate — have supported the Earl of Desmond's rebellion.

Art's son Dónal (Donald) became the O'Leary clan chief after the death of his uncle Donnchadh (Denis) in 1638. He was listed as occupant of the Carrignaneelagh tower house in the 1641 civil survey of the barony of Muskerry.

In 1650, Cromwellian troops occupied the tower house. They garrisoned the district and occupied the castle until shortly before the restoration of the Stuart monarchy with Charles II in 1660. They left the tower in poor shape.

During the eighteenth century, the Barry family acquired the neighbouring townland. They lived in a house adjoining the castle.

---

[8] *Tudor and Stuart Ireland*, by Margaret MacCurtain (Gill and Macmillan, 1972), p. 79.

[9] See Appendix B, Section VI.

James Barry (1761-1835), dubbed "Big Barry" by Mary O'Leary, earned a notorious reputation as one of the most grasping landlords in the district. In 1822, the year of the Keimaneigh battle in which Barry fought on the side of the English, his house was burned to the ground by members of the Whiteboy secret society of Catholic peasant farmers. The Whiteboys were known locally as the Rockites, after their outlaw leader, the mysterious Capt. Rock. Barry ordered his tenants to rebuild the house, using stone from Carrignaneelagh castle. The rebuilt farmhouse still stands, now divided into two separate dwellings, but there is no trace of the castle.

As for Barry, the story goes (according to Mary O'Leary's biographer, Fr. Donncha Ó Donnchú) that he was buried in 1835 in the old graveyard in Inchigeelagh on the same day that a female member of the O'Leary clan was buried there. After her graveside rituals were concluded, the O'Leary mourners gathered around Barry's tomb. One of them stomped on his flagstone and said, "Yes, there you are now as weak and feeble as the old woman we ourselves have brought. A bold man you were at the Battle of Keimaneigh, and now make the devil take your soul off with him."[10]

Before his death, about 1830, Barry built a road through the Pass of Keimaneigh at the point where the government militia had difficulties moving in their troops during the 1822 battle. In 1998, the Bantry and Ballingeary historical societies installed a monument at this location to commemorate those killed in the battle.

CASTLE AT CARRIGNACURRA

An earlier O'Leary castle was built, between 1450 and 1500, on a rock near the banks of the Lee, at a place called Carrignacurra (Rock of the Weir), about one mile southeast of the present township of Inchigeelagh. The letters "A.L." found on a wall of that castle would suggest that the builder was a clan member named Art O'Laoire. It stood five floors tall, with the top two floors serving as the family's private rooms. The ruins of this castle still stand. The founder of this branch of the clan was Diarmuid Óg (Dermot the Younger) O'Laoire, uncle of Carrignaneelagh chief Art O'Laoire, whose involvement in the Earl of Desmond's rebellions was somewhat more conspicuous than that of his nephew, Art. An inquisition held

---

[10] *Filíocht Mháire Bhuidhe Ní Laoghaire* by An tAthair Donncha Ó Donnchú, MA (Oifig an tSoláthair, 1931) p. 76.

in Shandon Castle, Cork, on 9 September 1588 ruled that Diarmuid Óg had been active in the Desmond revolts.

Diarmuid Óg, who lived at Carrignacurra from 1565 onward, named his first-born son Tadhg Meirgeach (Timothy the rusty, or the crusty one), and this dynastic clan-name — O'Laoire Meirgeach — passed to several of Tadhg's descendants. In 1584, a listing of the occupants at Carrignacurra included Diarmuid Óg and his wife Eileen, sons Tadhg and Donal, and daughter Ellen, along with thirteen soldiers — eighteen people in all.

Other dynastic clan-names associated with Inchigeelagh parish at that time include O'Laoire Art, O'Laoire Bolgaighe (of the smallpox), O'Laoire Breac (speckled), O'Laoire Cart (probably from Mac Art: son of Art), O'Laoire Bhuí (the yellow or the sallow), O'Laoire Céadach (possessing one hundred, likely cattle), O'Laoire Ceithearnach (kern-like), O'Laoire na Cipe (of the stock or block), O'Laoire Clogach (the blistered one), O'Laoire Dana (bold), O'Laoire Dorcha (dark one), O'Laoire Mocheirghe (of the early rising), O'Laoire Rua (red-haired), O'Laoire Glas (grey or pallid), O'Laoire Riabhach (brindled), O'Laoire Runtach (secretive).

The O'Laoire Bhuí branch, from which Mary O'Leary is descended, did not qualify for occupancy of any O'Leary castles. From the 1640s onward, the Clan Bhuí (sometimes anglicized as Boy) were associated primarily with the western townlands on either side of the Pass of Keimaneigh: Inchideraille, Derreenglass and Tooreennanean (Little Lea of the Birds), where Mary O'Leary was born in 1774. But, as can be seen from the names appearing in the various O'Leary wills of the seventeenth and eighteenth century, they did seem to develop some links with the O'Laoire Meirgeach line of Carrignacurra. In a closely-knit community like Iveleary, even those consigned to the outer limits of the clan power-sharing structure were still allowed a direct connection to the centre.

CASTLE AT DROMCARRA

A third O'Leary castle was built near Dromcarra, east of Carrignaneelagh, about six miles southwest of Macroom. It was badly damaged in 1650 during the Cromwellian campaign, but the ruins remained upright until 1968, when the local authorities condemned the structure as unsafe.

The first known owner was Donnchadh (Denis) O'Laoire, the younger brother of Art Mac Conchobhar O'Laoire of Carrignaneelagh who became clan chief in 1572.

Art served as chief for twenty years before passing the title to his brother Auliffe Ruadh (Humphrey the red-haired). Auliffe was killed in 1601 at the battle of Ahakeera, a tribal clash over cattle involving about one hundred O'Laoire clan members and members of the neighbouring O'Crowley clan of Dunmanway. The O'Laoire title then passed to Art's younger brother Donnchadh (Denis).

Donnchadh, known as an Ghaorthaí (the Geary), found himself competing for the Carrignaneelagh castle with Art's son Dónal (Donald), and eventually decided to build his own tower house at Dromcarra. A modest structure by castle standards, measuring 30 ft long by 20 ft wide with a height of 40 ft, Dromcarra was completed in 1625 at a cost of £110. Donnchadh lived there until his death in 1638. The castle then became the property of his son and heir Auliffe.

This castle was virtually destroyed during Lord Broghill's campaign in 1650, but managed to remain upright until 1968 when the Irish army demolished it in an explosives exercise.

GAELIC REVIVAL

The three O'Leary castles were all built before 1541, when the English Crown moved to suppress any ideas of religious or political independence in Ireland. At the same time, the Crown tried to recapture some of the ground it lost during the fourteenth and fifteenth centuries, when English political and cultural influence declined throughout the country.

Ireland had witnessed something of a Gaelic revival from the mid-1300s onward as the Crown became preoccupied, first with the Hundred Years' War against France (1337-1453), then with the subsequent thirty years of civil war during the Wars of the Roses (1457-87) when the English crown changed hands six times. These distractions created an opportunity for some of the more powerful Gaelic chieftains and Anglo-Norman lords to turn Ireland into a semi-autonomous feudal outpost.

In 1541, King Henry VIII moved to restore English dominance in Ireland. He assumed the title "king of Ireland," and called on all Irish rulers to swear allegiance to him. In the process, he effectively abolished the old Irish kingdoms. The Irish kings pledged allegiance without realizing that such a gesture meant signing away their lands to the Crown. Previously, pledging allegiance to the monarch had meant little more than ritual and pageantry. As soon as the English armies sailed back across the Irish Sea, the native rulers regained control of their territories. In this instance, however, swearing allegiance to the Crown marked the first step in the Tudor conquest of Ireland.

THE PLANTATION OF MUNSTER

It was left to Henry's daughter, Elizabeth I, who ascended to the throne in 1558, to carry through what her father had started. During the 1570s and 1580s, Elizabethan armies firmly established English rule in the southern Irish province of Munster and the western province of Connacht. Attempts to replace native landowners with English settlers, however, proved largely unsuccessful. The so-called Plantation of Munster failed because the estates were unwieldy and difficult to manage. Most of the Munster planters, including Sir Walter Raleigh and the poet Edmund Spenser, abandoned their holdings during the turmoil of the 1590s when a major rebellion in the northern province of Ulster by Hugh O'Neill, the earl of Tyrone, placed an almost intolerable strain on England's stretched resources.

It was during this period that the MacCarthy and O'Leary clans were able to regain some of their confiscated lands. They were pardoned for having taken up arms whenever they felt English expansion threatened their interests. They were also granted permission to hold land as long as they had no charges of murder or treason against them. One further condition of a 1573 pardon granted to Conchobhar O'Laoire, father of Carrignaneelagh branch founder Art O'Laoire, was that he surrender 131 cows to the English army stationed in Munster. In a country where wealth still tended to be measured in terms of cattle rather than land, this was a significant concession.

When the Scottish king James I, a Protestant, ascended to the English throne in 1603, many of the Catholic Irish leaders, including those of the MacCarthy and O'Leary clans, pledged allegiance to him. In return, they were allowed to take back more of their ancestral lands and — in the case of the MacCarthys — the titles that originally went with them. Donogh Mac Cormaic Óg MacCarthy, for example, was named both Baron of Blarney (1578) and Viscount of

Muskerry (1628). Occupancy of the lands hardly constituted clear ownership, however. MacCarthy's rent rose from £16 to £100 annually.

CROMWELLIAN CAMPAIGN BEGINS

Many of the MacCarthy and O'Leary land holdings were forfeited during the 1650s, when English officials took advantage of every legal pretext to dispossess Irish Catholic landowners. The situation became most critical when Oliver Cromwell, named Lord Protector after the execution of King Charles I, gave the Catholic landowners of Munster, Leinster and western Ulster the option of going "to hell or to Connacht." By this he meant that, under penalty of death no Irish could live east of the River Shannon, and only those who could prove they had not been rebels could own land west of the Shannon. Donogh MacCarthy, the Gaelic lord of Muskerry, surrendered his estates and fled into exile.

In 1641, eight years before Cromwell landed in Dublin, Catholics owned more than 60 percent of the profitable land in Ireland. In the Inchigeelagh area, the clan of O'Laoire Bhuí held eight townlands. By 1659, the figure for Catholic land ownership had dropped to about 8 percent, with most of the owners living in Connacht. A series of penal laws were subsequently enacted, prohibiting Catholics from owning land at all.

The 1654 Civil Survey of the barony of Muskerry depicts Iveleary as utterly devastated by the Cromwellian campaign. The tower-houses in Carrignacurra and Dromcarra were badly damaged, and English soldiers garrisoned the castle at Carrignaneelagh. A massive disruption of the old order had ensued.

With the restoration of the Stuart monarchy with Charles II in 1660, many of the dispossessed Gaelic lords were allowed to take back at least a portion of their estates. Donogh MacCarthy returned to Ireland and was named Earl of Clancarthy in 1660 — five years before his death — because of his ancestral claim to the Gaelic overlordship of all Muskerry. After his death in 1665, his wife Eileen assumed possession of his estates.

The O'Learys, having lost their previous status as semi-independent landowners, became tenants of Clancarthy — an arrangement that failed to suit many of them. Some moved to County Clare, others spread their wings with the Wild Geese — the name traditionally given to the Irish who have migrated to other countries

— and others became outlaws in the mountains. The main Carrignaneelagh branch eventually moved to Drishane and Millstreet.

Some members of the O'Leary clan did, nevertheless, manage to retain some hold on their Iveleary homeland. One who successfully claimed restoration of his lands in 1699, for example, was Capt. Céadach (Keadagh) O'Leary of Teergay, a clansman of the O'Laoire Meirgeach family of Carrignacurra. Keadagh's military title derived from his service as an officer in the army of King James II during the Williamite wars. He served in an infantry regiment led by Sir John Fitzgerald

The coronation of the Catholic King James II, in 1685, gave a much-needed boost to the hopes of Irish Catholics who had lost much of their profitable lands during the Cromwellian campaign of the 1650s. The English parliament, however, would not accept a return to Catholicism. The Dutch prince, William of Orange, replaced James in a bloodless coup.

James decided he could still rely on Irish Catholics if he attempted to regain his throne. In 1689, he landed in Cork and raised an army of 25,000 from the ranks of Irish Catholics. In 1690, James lost to the Williamite forces at the famous Battle of the Boyne, after which he fled to France. Irish Catholic resistance continued for more than a year. During this time, the MacCarthy and O'Leary clans lost possessions and status.

THE O'LEARYS BECOME OUTLAWS

The fortunes of Donogh MacCarthy, the fourth Earl of Clancarthy, rose and fell with James II. In 1690, he was charged with high treason, imprisoned, and sent into exile in Germany. His lands were all forfeited to the Crown. When pardoned by King George I in 1721, Clancarthy was given a stipend of £300 a year, but his lands remained the holdings of the English monarch. This confiscation of his estates scattered the O'Learys even further. Many of them took to the hills around Iveleary. Of those fourteen or so O'Leary clansmen who were still living in the area in 1694, many were branded by the English as outlaws, and the remainder were suspected of being "friends, relations, and harbourers of tories (outlaws)."[11]

---

[11] *Family Names of County Cork* by Diarmuid O'Murchadha (The Collins Press, 1996), p. 211.

This outlaw mentality seems to have been characteristic of the O'Learys. Despite the ravages of wars and confiscations, they continued to regroup, move forward, and challenge the authority of the English usurpers. As Diarmuid O'Murchadha wrote in his book, *Family Names of County Cork*:

> The speed and tenacity with which the local population re-established itself is surely a testimony to that sturdy independence which had permeated the way of life in Iveleary for many generations.
>
> It is hardly a coincidence that from this one remote upland parish emanated some of the most notable of what might be termed anti-establishment personages and events throughout succeeding centuries, incidents which in Gaelic folk-memory have always had a symbolic impact far above and beyond their historical significance.

Munster's most widely known, and perhaps most lamented folk hero of the eighteenth century, Art O'Leary, asserted a proud claim to this anti-establishment tradition of Iveleary. His father, Conchobhar O'Leary of Ballymurphy (near Crossbarry), was one of the signatories to the 1753 will of Conchobhar Meirgeach O'Leary ("Cornl. O'Leary of Carrignacurra, Gentleman"), which indicates a strong Iveleary connection. [12]

The following century saw the famous Whiteboy action in Keimaneigh, when an English soldier was killed by Séamus Walsh and Conchobhar (Conor) Bhuí O'Leary, brother of Mary O'Leary. Walsh was hanged by the English for his part in that skirmish but Conchobhar Bhuí O'Leary was acquitted.

Some time before that, the English government had sowed the seeds of enduring future discontent when it established a commission to deal with the ancestral lands taken from the Irish chieftains.

The Whiteboys evolved during the 1760s as a secret society of Catholic peasant farmers formed to secure summary justice for issues ranging from the enclosure of commonages (common land for pasturing animals), to rack rents (exorbitant six-monthly increases),

---

[12] See Appendix B, IV, below.

to the payment of tithes (one-tenth of income) to the Protestant church.)[13]

In 1702, the English land commission sold all of Clancarthy's Muskerry properties for £181,460–8s.–4d to The Hollow Sword Blade Corporation, a firearms manufacturing company that had supplied arms to the soldiers of King William during the war against James II. The English government owed the company £97,000. This debt was taken into consideration when the selling price for the lands was established.

In 1721, Clancarthy regained his title but not his estates. His son Robert, a warship captain, tried in 1734 to regain the estates, but to no avail. He died in 1770 at age 84, and the Clancarthy titles died with him.

THE O'LEARYS LOSE CARRIGNACURRA

As the Clancarthy fortunes declined, so did those of the O'Learys. They lost their much-battered castle at Carrignacurra, already damaged by the Cromwellian invasion, when it was taken over by the soldiers of King William in the 1690s. During this military occupation, the structure fell into further disrepair. The castle subsequently became the property of the Hollow Sword Blade Corporation, which later resold it to an Englishman named Masters.

A description of the Carrignacurra castle, the ruins of which are still standing, was offered by Cork historian John Windele after he visited Inchigeelagh in 1850:

> A mural (circular) staircase at NW angle, the building roofed, but roof in bad repair. The chambers extremely dark. Many of the windows walled up. The interior arched. The Bower room quite plain and unornamented. No mantelpiece in the great capacious fireplace, whether ever? Gone at all events. SE angle of the castle has one of those strange projecting spurs as at Mashanaglass Castle. It is perforated with slit or shot."[14]

---

[13] *Peasants and Power: The Whiteboy Movements and their Control in Pre-Famine Ireland,* by Michael Beames (St. Martins Press, 1983).

[14] Excerpt from the 1996 Journal of the Ballingeary Historical Society.

After losing the castle, the head of the O'Leary clan, Conchobhar Meirgeach O'Laoire (Cornelius the Rusty) still retained leases on the Carrignacurra lands, plus the townland of Tooreennanean, where Mary O'Leary was born. Conchobhar Meirgeach willed these leases to his infant sons Diarmuid (Jeremiah) and Cornelius Jr. when he died in 1699. Because they were minors, they were entrusted to the guardianship of their clansman Capt. Céadach (Keadagh) O'Leary of Teergay, a shrewd acquisitor who combined the Carrignacurra lands with leases assembled from other O'Learys.

The two sons of Conchobhar Meirgeach O'Laoire eventually recovered their leases from Céadach, in return for a payment of £127 1s 11d to Céadach. One of the sons, Cornelius Jr., eventually assumed possession of the lands, which he willed to his son Timothy in 1753.

At about the same time, Mary O'Leary's ancestors, who had held the eastern townland of Inchideraille and the western townland of Derreenglass — on either side of the Pass of Keimaneigh — for more than one hundred years, acquired the townland of Tooreennanean, halfway between.

What little that was left of Tooreennanean, amounting to about fifty acres after being divided and subdivided among clan members, eventually passed to Mary O'Leary's father, Diarmuid Bhuí O'Laoire, who was born there in 1751.

THE FAMILY OF DIARMUID BHUÍ O'LAOIRE

Diarmuid Bhuí O'Laoire and his wife Siobhán (Joanna) raised three daughters and five sons on their fifty-acre farm in the townland of Tooreennanean, near the Pass of Keimaneigh in West Cork. Mary O'Leary, born 1774, was the eldest. The others were Diarmuid, Tadhg (Timothy), Seán, Conchobhar (Cornelius), Neil (Ellen), Risteárd (Richard) and Nóra. They were a good-looking, fun-loving family, according to songs composed by sons Diarmuid and Tadhg:

> I cannot gainsay it — I'm lively and carefree
> For that is the way with O'Leary Clan Bhuí. *(Diarmuid)*

> A thirst greatly plagues me, and with cards I am keen
> With the 'five' and with tables (backgammon) as good as you've seen
> Ships laden from Spain, here safely I'd steer
> And a curse on the barmaid, my plea she won't hear. *(Tadhg)*

Diarmuid Bhuí's eldest son Diarmuid was born in 1775. Diarmuid Bhuí gave him one-quarter of his land, 12.5 acres, and he settled there with his wife, the former Eibhlín Ní Chróinin (Ellen Cronin).

The younger Diarmuid's brother, Conchobhar (Cornelius or Conor), born in 1792, married a woman from the neighbouring Coakley family, and lived with her on another quarter, 12.5 acres, of Diarmuid Bhuí's land.

Son Tadhg (Timothy) married a woman from Bantry named Murphy. He leased a small farm that he subsequently lost during the famines of the 1840s. He spent the rest of his life as a travelling pedlar (tinker) in the area.

Risteárd (Richard), the youngest son, was born in 1795. He seems to have been a carefree soul without much purpose in his life beyond having a good time. ("A sporting blade," as biographer Ó Donnchú characterized him.) He never married or settled down.

Both Diarmuid Jr. and Conchobhar fell upon hard times, and moved back to their father's Tooreennanean property around 1820, when they defaulted on the rent on their inherited tenant lands. Conchobhar became a cattle herder. It is not known what happened to his wife. Conchobhar was listed without spouse in the 1821 census.

Daughter Neil married Tadhg O'Laoire from Rossmore, about two miles east of Inchigeelagh. Their descendants were still living there in the 1930s, when biographer Ó Donnchú completed his Mary O'Leary manuscript.

Youngest daughter Nóra lived in Inchideraille, west of Inchigeelagh, with her husband Dónal Ó Crochúr (Donal O'Connor). They were evicted during the famine and are both buried in Inchideraille.

A neighbour named Michael Murphy took possession of the lands abandoned by brothers Diarmuid Jr. and Conchobhar after they moved back with their parents. The rent, however, proved too much for Murphy, and he lost the property after living there for just two years.

According to the custom of the period, anyone who paid the back rent was then entitled to assume occupancy of the property. An opportunist named Donal O'Sullivan thus became the next occupant. He paid £24 in back rent, took possession of the farm and, perhaps predictably, found himself at loggerheads with both the dispossessed O'Learys and Michael Murphy. Mary O'Leary referred to the clash between Murphy (popularly known as *Móin* — literally, "of the bog") and O'Sullivan (popularly known as *Diomhaoin* — literally, "idle") in one verse:

> The Bright Lord of Glory knows contrast between
> the family of *Móin* and the Clan of *Diomhaoin*.

Of the dispute with the O'Learys, she sang:

> Come let us rout them! Come let us rout them!
> Come let us rout them, the Clan of *Diomhaoin!*
> Come let us rout them, pitiless bounders!
> Sad is the house of the Clan Laoire Bhuí.

After an encounter with O'Sullivan one Sunday at church, Mary O'Leary was moved to declare:

> An ignorant lout is Donal Diomhaoin
> Bandy-legged tout, unmanly and mean;
> A young heifer's milk to drink he'd not dream

But take it to sell up and down the boreen (lane).

O'Sullivan responded in kind:

> You lie, you bragging old hag of Clan Bhuí
> He and his kind far outclass your entire breed
> They're kindly, large-hearted with plenty to eat
> And none of them ever had to live in a creel (barrel).

The feud came to a head when Donal O'Sullivan was attacked on a hillside one foggy night while walking home. The O'Learys were charged, convicted of assault, and some went to prison. The feud is believed to have ended with the death of Séamas de Búrca (Jimmy Burke) Mary O'Leary's second son. Another of Mary O'Leary's sons, accompanied by a neighbour, travelled to Inchigeelagh after the funeral to dig the grave. On their way home, their horse spooked, suffered a seizure, and fell dead on the roadway. Burke was reluctant to seek help, but did suggest that his companion might ask a brother of Donal O'Sullivan — who happened to live nearby—about borrowing a horse. This man, as it turned out, was happy to loan the pair one of his horses. His Good Samaritan act is said to have helped resolve the differences between the families. "Quarrels have periods of abstinence," commented biographer Ó Donnchú. The O'Sullivan family continued to occupy Tooreennanean in the years thereafter.

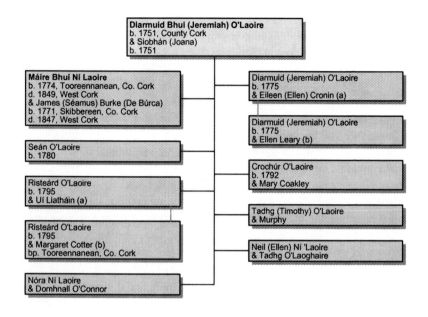

Diarmuid Bhuí (Jeremiah) O'Laoire
b. 1751, County Cork
& Siobhán (Joana)
b. 1751

Máire Bhuí Ní Laoire
b. 1774, Tooreennanean, Co. Cork
d. 1849, West Cork
& James (Séamus) Burke (De Búrca)
b. 1771, Skibbereen, Co. Cork
d. 1847, West Cork

Seán O'Laoire
b. 1780

Risteárd O'Laoire
b. 1795
& Uí Liatháin (a)

Risteárd O'Laoire
b. 1795
& Margaret Cotter (b)
bp. Tooreennanean, Co. Cork

Nóra Ní Laoire
& Domhnall O'Connor

Diarmuid (Jeremiah) O'Laoire
b. 1775
& Eileen (Ellen) Cronin (a)

Diarmuid (Jeremiah) O'Laoire
b. 1775
& Ellen Leary (b)

Crochúr O'Laoire
b. 1792
& Mary Coakley

Tadhg (Timothy) O'Laoire
& Murphy

Neil (Ellen) Ní 'Laoire
& Tadhg O'Laoghaire

MARY O'LEARY AND HER FAMILY

Mary O'Leary was born in 1774. She lived at home until 1792 when, at age eighteen, she ran away with and married Séamus de Búrca (James Burke). He came from Skibbereen, and made his living as a horse trader. During one of his many trips to horse fairs in the Keimaneigh area he met Mary, and was smitten. They eloped to Skibbereen, married, bought a small farm near Ballingeary, settled there, prospered, and established a reputation for being extraordinarily generous with their hospitality. A crossing on the River Lee, near where they lived, became known as the Ford of the Burkes.

Over time, James and Mary amassed tenant land holdings of 150 acres southwest of Ballingeary in the townlands of Inchibeg and Inchimore, ("all the Inches," as biographer Ó Donnchú puts it) overlooking Keimaneigh. They relocated to Inchimore, and all of their nine children were born there. They became quite wealthy. They lived in a comfortable home on the banks of the Lee, had ten men working for them, and maintained a fine herd of cattle, along with horses that they used for both work and recreation.

Their neighbours reported that wealth never caused the Burkes to lose touch with those less fortunate than themselves. They were widely known for helping the poorer people of the area. As biographer Ó Donnchú says, "they never lost the old spirit, and never failed to be moved to compassion by a poor man's plea. They kept an open house for all, through good times and bad."

James and Mary raised six sons and three daughters. In chronological order, they were Seán (John), Séamas (James), Micheál (Michael), Risteárd (Richard), Eilic (Alec), Pádraig (Patrick), Neil (Ellen), Máire (Mary) and Siobhán (Joanna).

Seán, born in 1793, married Nóra Ní Chróinin (Honna Cronin) from Gorteennakilla, north of Ballingeary, in 1818. They had six sons and three daughters. They lived with Seán's parents until their second son, Risteárd (Richard), was born, at Christmas 1819. At that point, Seán and Nóra acquired some of the Inchibeg property from James and Mary, built a home, and raised their family. Eventually, they were evicted from the Inchibeg property for defaulting on their rent, and moved several miles southwest to the parish of Scoile

(Schull). Seán died a relatively young man. Biographer Ó Donnchú suggests he may have been one of the Whiteboys hanged after the Battle of Keimaneigh, although his name does not appear in any official documents. Two of Mary O'Leary's poems, *Tuireamh Sheáin de Búrc* ("Lament for John Burke") and *Caoineadh Sheáin de Búrc*, ("The 'Keening' of John Burke") are variations on a lament for her dead son. In *Tuireamh*, she sings:

> My three brothers have travelled, their horses are exhausted,
> Two from London and the third from Ireland with writs duly sealed,
> Bringing from the King a free pardon for you.

Ó Donnchú says this verse suggests that three of Burke's brothers-in-law travelled to England and obtained a pardon from the King, but failed to arrive back in time to save him from the gallows. If he was not executed for Whiteboy activity, it is possible that he may have hanged for committing highway robbery. A man named Burke (first name unknown) was hanged for such a crime at Gallows Green in Cork city on 21 September 1822.

Séamas, the second son of James and Mary, was born in 1794. He is reputed to have been very wild ("quite rakish," as Ó Donnchú puts it) as a young man. He married circa 1833 Gobnait de Búrca (Abbey Burke) from the Macroom area. James and Mary gave him tenancy rights to part of their Inchimore property, and a couple of cows to get him started as a farmer.

Micheál (Michael), the third son, was born in 1796. In 1819, he married Neil Ní Shúilleabháin (Nell O'Sullivan) from Bantry. They had two sons, Seán and Séamas, and six daughters. They lived in Inchibeg for some years and then, following a familiar pattern of the times, were evicted for defaulting on the rent. Micheál left for the United States. He returned to Ireland several times, and died at Clogher, a few miles south of Inchigeelagh.

Risteárd, the fourth son, was born in 1798. In 1829 he married Siobhán Ní Cheallacháin (Joanna Callaghan) from Macroom. His father gave him tenancy rights to the northern half of Inchimore. They had seven children. Eventually, they too were evicted and lived in the United States for some years. Their youngest son, Alexander, born 1842, went into the brick manufacturing trade in Chicago. He did well financially, visited Ireland several times, and installed a headstone for his parents on their grave in the old churchyard at Inchigeelagh. The inscription, in English, reads as follows:

Pray for the repose of the souls of
Richard Burke
and his wife Johanna Callaghan
of Inchibeg R.I.P.
Erected to their memory
by their loving son
Alexander Burke
Chicago, USA

Alexander died in Chicago in 1914. He left money for an altar to be installed in the church at Inchigeelagh, a structure now in ruins. He left a wife and eleven children. One of the children, Richard, became a justice of the peace. Another son, Alexander Jr., became a doctor.

James and Mary's fifth son, Alec, was born in 1804. He married Mary Callaghan from Kilmicheal in 1842. They lived in Inchimore and had eight children: John, Michael, Eileen, Brigid, James, Siobhán, Richard and Alec. Oldest son John was the father of Johanna (Hannah) Burke, who married Michael Twomey of Ballyvourney in 1913. She was my maternal grandmother.

Patrick, the sixth son of James and Mary, was a big hearty man and not very intelligent. ("Not too coherent in himself," as Ó Donnchú puts it.) He spent most of his life living with his brother Alec and family.

Daughter Neil married Conchobhar Ó hÁiligheasa (Cornelius Hallassey) of nearby Toohandroman. Daughter Máire married Tadhg O'Laoire Brady (Timothy O'Leary Brady) of Gortafludig, just north of Keimaneigh. Daughter Siobhán married Dónal Burke of Oileán Faoide (Whiddy Island).

The landlord for the Inchimore and Inchibeg properties was a Captain Wallace who lived in Macroom. He died accidentally when he fell through the window of a bank. When his brother, his only surviving relative, heard of the captain's misfortune, he succumbed as well — from shock! That left the Wallace properties intestate. The land was auctioned off, and the Pope family from Waterford bought in. They upped the total rent on the Inchimore and Inchibeg properties to £140 a year. The Burkes also owed £100 to a Cork butter merchant named Donal O'Sullivan. Money woes were thus to plague the Burkes for the next twenty years. Despite this, they continued to keep an open house for their neighbours, even though they could ill afford it.

Between the 1820s and the 1840s, the Burke cattle and farming business went into a steady decline. These were the years leading up to the Great Famine, when an unknown, uncontrollable blight turned Ireland's potato crop into foul slime. Tenant farmers who raised cattle and grain for export, while depending for subsistence on potatoes, found their precarious, meager existence — their very lives — in danger. The potato crop failed initially in 1818 and again in 1821, with further famines occurring from 1845 onward.

The worst year of all was 1847. That was when the bailiffs arrived and evicted James and Mary and son Alec and family from Inchimore. The introduction of rents on previously unfarmed areas followed by a succession of dramatic increases in these levies had created severe economic hardship for James and Mary and their children. Son Michael, however, received a lucky break when the rent on his Inchibeg property was lowered by £5. That allowed him to continue living there, and to take in his parents and younger brother Alec and family, when they were banished from Inchimore.

Mary O'Leary died in 1849, a year or so after she and husband James were forced to move in with their son Michael. One of her last poems is thought to have been a lament for someone who left the Catholic faith and became a Protestant:

> Oh Donagh, the report has filled me with anguish
> That you have turned from the fold and joined the speakers
> of English.

After she died, she was interred in what is now the old churchyard at Inchigeelagh, where other members of the Burke family also lie buried. An elaborate gravestone commemorating Mary O'Leary and her husband was installed in 1995 by Nan Burke O'Donovan, a direct descendant of Mary O'Leary's oldest son, Seán.

The Burke farm at Inchimore accrued to a Seán Rua Breathnach (John Roe Walsh) when he paid off the rent arrears. Twenty years or so later, a Conchobhar Ó Luasa (Conor Lucey) from Ballyvourney acquired the place. No members of the Burke family were left living at Inchimore after the famine.

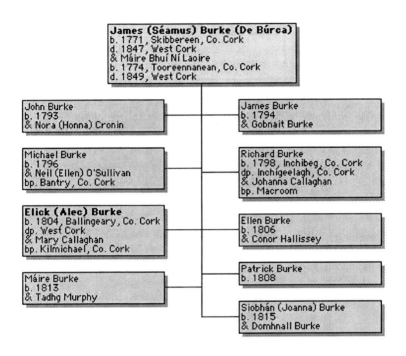

James (Séamus) Burke (De Búrca)
b. 1771, Skibbereen, Co. Cork
d. 1847, West Cork
& Máire Bhuí Ní Laoire
b. 1774, Tooreennanean, Co. Cork
d. 1849, West Cork

John Burke
b. 1793
& Nora (Honna) Cronin

James Burke
b. 1794
& Gobnait Burke

Michael Burke
b. 1796
& Neil (Ellen) O'Sullivan
bp. Bantry, Co. Cork

Richard Burke
b. 1798, Inchibeg, Co. Cork
dp. Inchigeelagh, Co. Cork
& Johanna Callaghan
bp. Macroom

Elick (Alec) Burke
b. 1804, Ballingeary, Co. Cork
dp. West Cork
& Mary Callaghan
bp. Kilmichael, Co. Cork

Ellen Burke
b. 1806
& Conor Hallissey

Patrick Burke
b. 1808

Máire Burke
b. 1813
& Tadhg Murphy

Siobhán (Joanna) Burke
b. 1815
& Domhnall Burke

THE FAILED IRISH UPRISING

When Mary O'Leary was a child during the 1770s, King George III was faced with the rebellion of the North American colonies. The American Revolution forced the British government to withdraw nearly all of its troops from Ireland, and place the defence of the country in the hands of so-called "Volunteers" — non-professional militia units drawn from the ranks of the Anglo-Irish. In the Inchigeelagh area of West Cork, the Volunteers — between sixty and one hundred of them — were led by Jasper Masters, a landlord who had inherited from his grandfather the ancestral castle at Carrignacurra that belonged to the O'Leary clan up to the 1690s.[15]

The stabilizing presence of this Anglo-Irish militia left England comfortable enough during the American war to briefly concede wider powers to the Irish parliament. In 1782, the Westminster government forfeited its right to make laws for Ireland. This hardly amounted to a ratification of Irish independence, however. The Catholic majority continued to be denied political participation. Within two decades, both the native Irish and British government would decide that continued political control of Ireland by the Anglo-Irish—the Ascendancy—was both impractical and intolerable.

During the 1790s, Britain went to war against France. A group of Irish radicals, led by the Protestant barrister Theobald Wolfe Tone, saw this as an opportunity for bringing about significant changes in the way Ireland was governed. In 1796, Tone travelled to France and persuaded the ruling Directory that French-backed rebellion in Ireland could be a first step toward a French military victory over the English. The subsequent establishment of a republican government in the British Isles would further the cause of democratic reform in Ireland.

To this end, in December 1796, fifteen thousand French troops under the leadership of General Lazare Hoche set sail for Ireland. Tone, who travelled with the expedition, had arranged beforehand that a general uprising in Ireland would accompany the French landing at Bantry Bay in southwest County Cork. The poets of

---

[15] *A Military History of Ireland,* edited by Thomas Bartlett and Keith Jeffery (Cambridge University Press, 1996)

Munster generally applauded this venture. Mary O'Leary's contribution to the cause was a poem entitled *Ar Leacain na Gréine* (On a Sunny Hillside) in which she expressed hope that when the French arrived England would be defeated and the United Irishmen would gain dominance. The United Irishmen were a political reform society founded in Belfast by Tone and driven underground by the English when it became apparent that the organization had links with the French radicals. Here's how Mary O'Leary described the pending arrival of the French in her poem:

> To each one that you see, give the news that they are coming.
> They are coming in force with powder and bullets and gun.
> Stout-hearted supporters, hastening — Louis[16] and the
> Spaniard[17] — as one.
> To Banba's[18] green shore they are coming, without delay, by
> the grace of God's son.

In the song *Fáinne an Lae* ("The Dawning of the Day") she added:

> Would you like to come into this inn
> and share friendship with me for a while?
> The answer she gave: "I cannot stop, for it is Harvest Day.
> The Duke of York[19] and his troops are being ravaged
> by the true Prince of the Gael
> And in one year more the boors will lie prostrate.
> That is the true account of my tidings.

Additionally, she sang, in the song, *Seó Leó, A Thoil* ("So Hush, My Love"):

> By next year, the boors will be grieving,

---

[16] Louis — Louis XVI of France. His name is intended to signify military aid from France.

[17] The Spaniard — indicating the whole nation of Spain. At that time, England was waging war against France, Spain and the Netherlands. Ireland would depend on military aid from these countries if it were to wage war with England.

[18] Poetic name for Ireland.

[19] The Duke of York — leader of the English in the war against France in 1793.

and the city streets will be free of smoke and fog.
You will have a gift I have not told you of yet:
The Duke's daughter in your chimney corner to amuse you.
So hush, my love, and cry no more.

The Hoche expedition was a failure. Fog and storms combined to disperse the armada many nautical miles short of their intended destination. Only fourteen of the forty-three ships managed to get anywhere close to Bantry Bay. Weather conditions remained so bad that even these ships opted to return to France rather than risk a landing. Along with them went any real hope of a successful Irish rebellion. Mary O'Leary articulated the nation's disappointment in her song "On a Sunny Hillside:"

My warrior sweet, of the Fleet do not talk to me any more.
So distressful to me is the grief it has brought to our shore.
The winds blew so fiercely over the deep that it sent many of them astray.
And in shackles they now sit, as happened to the regal lady[20] long ago.

The failed Hoche expedition was followed by a series of other unsuccessful revolts in 1797-8 when Catholic tenant farmers in Wexford wreaked vengeance upon their Protestant overlords, and Presbyterian farmers and linen workers in Antrim and Down protested the British connection. A small French force of one thousand men was defeated by the British in Mayo in August 1798. The following month, another French fleet was defeated at sea, off the coast of Donegal. Among the prisoners taken was Wolfe Tone. Brought to Dublin for trial, he took his own life while awaiting execution.

The 1798 rebellion, though a failure, is usually considered one of the great milestones of Irish history. It saw the concept of nationalism introduced for the first time to the general population. Up to that point, the word "Irish" had merely implied membership of a particular social group. Now, for the first time, it had definite political connotations. The pike, the colour green, and the songs of a nationalist balladeer like Mary O'Leary all became potent symbols of

---

[20] Regal lady — the Queen of England, possibly Anne Boleyn, the executed second wife of Henry VIII.

this new force. During the years after the rebellion, the leaders of such agrarian rebel groups as the Whiteboys and the Rockites would take to identifying themselves as United Irishmen commanders to show that they were following in the footsteps of Wolfe Tone.

THE BATTLE OF KEIMANEIGH

Mary O'Leary's most famous poem, *Cath Céim an Fhia* ("The Battle of Keimaneigh"), is in the repertoire of many West Cork balladeers. It was once described, by a teacher of Cork family historian Mary Casey, as the "finest piece of poetry in any known language."

The battle wasn't really a battle in the true sense, but rather a series of skirmishes. However, there were serious repercussions. Thirty-six of the participants were sentenced to be hanged following affrays in Carriganima, Deshure and Newmarket, as well as at Keimaneigh. Members of Mary O'Leary's family were forced to go on the run. Biographer Fr. Donncha Ó Donnchú suggests that her son John Burke may have been one of those executed. He says that her outspoken and lofty sentiments, as expressed in her poem, did no favours for her family.

The poem describes the 1822 armed clash between local militia troops and a secret society of Catholic tenant farmers, known as the Whiteboys, who took up arms to protest the payment of tithe rents for the upkeep of the Protestant church. The militia units were raised by local Protestant gentry and equipped at their expense, as protection against these insurgent Catholic peasants.

Economic conditions for Catholic tenant farmers and labourers were woeful in 1822. Arbitrary rent increases and evictions were the order of the day. A worldwide depression followed the defeat of Napoleon. West Cork was particularly hard hit by the loss of a lucrative market supplying butter and other provisions to ships docked in Cork harbour.[21]

The Whiteboys were one of several secret societies — groups of frustrated tenants and laborers — that used intimidation, arson, and sometimes armed force against their landlord bosses. They saw the landlords as being the embodiment of British rule in Ireland because

---

[21] "The Battle of Keimaneigh," by Peter O'Leary, published in the 1993 edition of the Ballingeary Historical Society Journal.

the landlords selected the grand juries, the local magistrates, and tithe proctors, and seemed to wield unlimited power.

"Their conduct of justice left the impression upon the minds of the common people that there was no law for them but the will of the magistrates," wrote a Skibbereen priest, Fr. M. Collins, in 1825. "The tithe proctor was above the law, and the tithe payer outside it."[22]

The Whiteboys operated in groups of twenty or thirty, coming out at night and returning to their homes before dawn. They tended to be most active in relatively prosperous areas where the tenants could appreciate the difference between good and lean years. In the Inchigeelagh area, they were known as the "Rockites" because their leader was a mysterious individual, real name unknown, who sent his followers notices bearing the signature, "John Rock, commander-in-chief of the United Irishman." Fr. Ó Donnchú suggests he was likely the son of someone who participated in the failed 1798 rebellion.

While they sometimes terrorized exceptionally venal landlords and their agents, the Whiteboys usually attacked tithe proctors — agents of the Church of Ireland — who collected "contributions" from all Irish people, regardless of religion. The attacks, however, were limited by the short supply of available weapons. A contemporary document describes the Whiteboy situation as follows:

> One of the most important practical limitations on the extent and development of the Whiteboy movement was the lack of arms in the hands of the peasantry. Consequently, every major outbreak was characterized by the plunder of arms from the houses of the gentry and richer farmers, creating in the minds of the authorities 'the frightful picture of an armed peasantry and disarmed gentry.' The arms obtained in this way were, however, limited in number, and the problems of maintaining them in good order and obtaining ammunition remained.
>
> Between 15 and 27 December 1821, for instance, Whiteboys raided some thirty-seven houses in the area around Bandon in Co. Cork and obtained only twenty-five guns, eight pistols, and a few swords and bayonets. The arms thus obtained were suitable for a small party raiding a

---

[22] Quoted by Peadar O'Donovan in the *Southern Star* newspaper, 19 August 1995.

farmhouse, or laying an ambush for an assassination, but they were completely inadequate in attempts to escalate the disturbances and take on forces of armed police or soldiers.

In an incident in southwest Cork in January 1822 between a patrol of fourteen soldiers and about three hundred insurgents, only some fourteen muskets were in the hands of the latter. One of these had been taken from one of the soldiers, who was 'cut off, surrounded, knocked down, and barbarously beaten.'[23]

The Pass of Keimaneigh, where the Rockites battled the soldiers of the Muskerry Blue Light Dragoons, is a route through the Shehy Mountains, between the summits of Bealick and Foilastookeen, in the middle of prosperous sheep-farming country, near the valley of Gougane Barra (St. Finbarr's mountain hollow), on the road between Macroom and Bantry. At the time Mary O'Leary composed her poem, the Pass was a narrow sheep path meandering beneath overhanging crags, providing good cover for hiding clansfolk.

The Battle of Keimaneigh occurred after the Rockite arms raids in the Bandon area during December 1821. The Rockites suspected afterwards that they might have been recognized and then followed. They established a lookout near the Pass to watch for approaching soldiers. When the warning signal was given, after a ten-day wait, the Rockites prepared for battle.

Accounts differ as to how the battle actually started. Some historians believe the Rockites ambushed the militia as they neared the Pass. Others think the soldiers were already lying in waiting there, and that the soldiers fired the first shots. Regardless, the historians generally agree that, some time during the early stages of the confrontation, two Rockites — Amhlaoibh (Auliffe or Humphrey) Lynch from nearby Derry, in the parish of Toohandroman, and Barry O'Leary from Garryantornora — were killed.

The battle then began in earnest, with some of the participants involved in one-on-one clashes. Whiteboy Séamus Walsh from Tooreenduff (immediately northeast of Tooreennanean) ran out of

---

[23] Extract from a dispatch from Wellesley to Sidmouth, 11 Jan 1822. *Papers relating to the Disturbed State of Ireland, Parliamentary Papers 1822* (2), xiv, p 5, and extract from a dispatch from Wellesley to Peel, 27 Jan. 1822, ibid. pp. 12-15.

ammunition at one point, and used the butt of his gun to fell a soldier named John Smith, while Smith — who had also run out of bullets — was loading buttons from his coat into his musket barrel.

"Oh, mercy, boys! Mercy," cried Smith as Conchobhar Bhuí O'Laoire, a brother of Mary O'Leary, joined Walsh.

"Let the devil give you mercy," replied Conchobhar Bhuí, grabbing Smith's bayonet and finishing him off with it. Conchobhar was subsequently charged with murder but acquitted.

The Rockites continued to command the Pass of Keimaneigh for a few weeks afterwards, then quietly returned to their homes and farms. "Probably they realized they had made their protest, and that there was not much more they could do," wrote Peter O'Leary in the *Ballingeary Historical Society Journal.* "Possibly they were influenced by the thoughts of the reprisals which were certain to follow."

There was no immediate improvement in the economic plight of the tenant farmers and labourers following the reprisals, which included some hangings. However, the Rockites did achieve a victory of sorts, some time afterwards, when the hated tithes were eliminated.

Mary O'Leary's poem "The Battle of Keimaneigh" contains all the colour and graphic description that comes from her having witnessed the battle while it was in progress:

I

Cois abhann Ghleanna an Chéama i nUíbh Laoghaire 'sea bhímse,
mar a dtéann an fia san oíche chun síorchodladh sóil.
Ag machnamh seal liom féinig ag déanamh mo smaointe, ag
éisteacht i gcoillte le binnghuth na néin.
Nuair a chuala an cath ag teacht aniar, is glór na n-each ag teacht le
sians.
Le fuaim an airm do chrith an sliabh, is níor bhinn linn a nglór.
Thánadar go naimhdeach mar a tiocfa gárda de chona ní.
Is mo chumhasa na sárfhir do fágadh faoi bhrón.

II

Níor fhan bean ná páiste i mbun áitribh ná tí acu ach na gártha do bhí
acu agus mílte olagón ag féachaint ar an ngárda ag teacht láidir 'na
dtimpeall.
Ag lámhach is ag líonadh is ag scaoileadh 'na dtreo, an liú gur lean a
bhfad i gcian.
Sé dúirt gach flaith gur mhaith leis triall: "Gluaisigí mear tá an cath
dá rian agus téimis 'na chomhair."
Thánadar na sárfhir i gcoim áthais le Clanna Gaeil is chomáineadar
na páintigh le fánaidh ar seol.

III

Is gairid dúinn go dtáinig lámh láidir ár dtimpeall do sheol amach ár
ndaoine go fíor-mhoch fén gceo.
An Barrach 'na bhumbháille, Barnet agus Beecher, Hedges agus
Faoitigh is na mílte eile leo.
Rí na bhfeart, go lagaidh iad gan chlú, gan mheas, gan rath, gan séan
i dtinte teasa a measc na bpian gan faoiseamh go deo!
Céad moladh mór le hÍosa nár dhíolamair as
an dtóir,
Ach bheith ag déanamh grinn de is 'á insint ar só.

I (*Translated by Donnchadh O'Luasaigh*)

Near the river bank in Keimaneigh in Iveleary I spend my time,
where the deer comes nightly for its restful repose.
Thinking for a while, pondering some memories, listening in the
woodlands to the birds' melodious tones.
From the west came the sound of battle of horses' hooves, of
armour's rattle, which quaked the hills in displeasing fashion,
loathsome to report.
So they came viciously like a pack of venomous hounds. I pity those
valiant men for whom no leader can be found.

II

Not a man, woman or child was left in their dwelling or house
without grief-cries and thousands of wailings as they watched the
guard vigorously surrounding them.
Shooting and loading and firing in their direction, the cry that went
out far and wide.
It was what every prince who wished to be on the move said: "Move
fast, the battle is being fought and let us go to meet it."
The heroes joined the Clanna Gael at a mountain recess, and they
drove the fat rabble away down the slope.

III

Short was the time until a strong hand surrounded us and led out our
people into the fog of early morning.
Barry[24] the bum-bailiff (was there), Barnet and Beecher, Hedges and
White and thousands of others besides.
O King of Great Deeds, may they be cast down into fires of heat, in
the midst of pain, without remission for all eternity!
A hundred great praises to Jesus that we didn't pay the penalty for
the rout,
But lived to make a joke of it, and tell the story at our ease.

---

[24] Barry — James Barry, or "Big Barry" as he was known, was the much-hated bailiff, tithe collector, landlord and high sheriff of the county. He lived at Carrignaneelagh, one of the ancestral properties of the O'Learys. He was very powerful, and a determined oppressor of the poor. He fought on the side of the English at the Battle of Keimaneigh, and continued to pursue the Rockites afterwards. He willed his properties to his son Nicholas. He lies buried in the old graveyard in Inchigeelagh.

47

IV

Is an bhliain seo anois atá againn beidh rás ar gach smíste,
Cuirfam insa díg iad, dríb ortha is fóid.
Ní iarrfam cúirt ná stáitse, beidh árdchroch 'na suí again,
Agus an chnáib go slachtmhar snímhte le díolthas 'na gcomhair.
Is acu atá an tslat, is olc í a riail,
I gcóistíbh greanta is maith é a ngléas,
Gach sórd le caitheamh - fleadh agus féasta - ag béaraibh ar bórd,
Gurabh é deir gach údar cruinn liom sara gcríochna siad deire an
fhómhair
Ins a leabhar so Pastorína go ndíolfaid as an bpóit.

V

Do bhí Smith ar a thár anáirde ar árdleacain fhraoigh dhuibh.
Ba ghránda bhí a ghnaoi is gan taoinnte ar a thóin.
Nár bheire crích is fearr iad an t-ál so Chailbhin chaoithigh,
Nár ghéill riamh do Chríost, ach puimp agus póit.
Beidh na sluaíte fear ag teacht gan chiach ar longaibh meara, is fada
é a dtriall,
Is an Frangcach theas nár mheathluigh riamh i bhfaobhar is i gcór.
Beidh cathracha á stríocadh agus tinteacha á lasadh leo,
Tá an cáirde fada díolta is an líonrith 'na gcomhair.

VI

Is, a Chlanna Gael na n-áran, ná stánaigí is ná stríocaigí,
Is gearr anois gan mhoill go mbeidh críoch ar bhúr ngnó.
Tógaigí suas bhúr gcráiste, tá an t-ál so le díbirt,
Go hIfreann 'á dtíoradh idir thinteacha teo.
Bíodh bhúr bpící glana i gceart i ngléas
Téigí 'on chath, ná fanaigí siar,
Tá an chabhair ag teacht le toil ó Dhia. Agus léirigí na póirc. Sáithigí
isteach go dána, in áitreabh a dtáinig rómhaibh,
Is mithid díbh é fháil is tá an cairde maith go leor.

IV

In this present year of ours, every boor will be put to rout,
They will be knocked into the dikes, the gutter will be their shroud.
We won't hold court or inquest, the gallows is a-building,
And the rope with vengeance twisting for their ugly throats.
They have the power, 'tis ill they rule, they are well appointed in
coaches too.
All sorts of food have this bear's brood for partying with pleasure.
An authority has informed me that before the harvest ends
The prophet Pastorini[25] is declaring their measure.

V

Smith[26] lay belly down on the black-heathered heath.
His bare backside and ugly features were loathsome to behold.
May they come to no better end, those foreign cubs of Calvin's
Whose God was pomposity and not the Christ, I'm told.
Many men will fast approach using a ship of vast proportion,
And the French, down south, who are so stoic are ready for the fray.
Cities will be razed, fires will be flamed, payment is due, the
reckoning has come.

VI

Dear beloved sons of Erin, do not stop or retreat, for the task
undertaken will soon be complete.
Keep up the courage, those runts must be routed, in Hell-fires to
flounder and roasted apiece.
Have your long pikes cleaned and polished, go into battle, don't stay
from it.
Help is at hand, that is God's promise.
Pulverize these porks.[27] Regain possession of your ancestral abodes,
There to be seated and remain for evermore.

---

[25] In the early nineteenth century, many Catholics believed Pastorini's 1771
prophecy that Protestantism would be extinguished forever in 1825.
[26] John Smith — an English soldier killed at the Battle of Keimaneigh by
Séamus Walsh and Conchobhar O'Laoire, brother of Mary O'Leary.
[27] Porks —Mary O'Leary also used such epithets as "swine" and "boor" as
contemptuous terms for the English.

VII

Stadfad feasta 'em dhántaibh táim láimh leis an gcríneacht,
Tá iomarca 'en drochchroí agam do bhuidhin na mbolg mór.
Ní gean dom a thuille a rádh leo, nára fearrde don mbuidhín é,
Ach ár agus sceimhle go dtí ar a gcór.
Nára díon dóibh stad ar sheal dá ngléas.
Nára díon dóibh carraig, cnoc, ná sliabh,
Mar a mbíodh an seannach mear dá fhiadhach, agus a ghéim acu ar seol.
Beidh gach seairfhear croíúil is a phíce agus a sleá 'na dhóid
Gan súil le sásamh choidhche ná díol as go deo.

VII

I'll sing no more, I've grown too old.
I'm full of spite for that bellied pork.
I've no more to say, I don't like their way,
Raided and routed may that be their store.
May they have no respite in times of fight.
May they be roofless day and night, condemned to roam and taking flight
Like the game they oftentimes drove.
Every hearty country-boy whose pikes and spears are raised on high
Will ne'er be fully satisfied in the settling of their score.

Rockite Humphrey Lynch was buried in Ballyvourney. Barry O'Leary was buried in the old graveyard at Inchigeelagh. Local lore suggests that as many as ten other Rockites were killed, including Michael Casey of Derryfineen. Of the thirty-six Rockites sentenced to be hanged, only a handful were actually executed. One was William Ring from Keamcorravooly, for whom Mary O'Leary composed the lament, *Caoineadh ar Liam Ó Rinn*. ("Lament for William Ring.") Another may have been Mary O'Leary's son, John Burke. Other Rockites received reprieves and were transported to Van Diemen's Land (Tasmania).

Mary O'Leary's lament for Ring begins:

> Women are wailing in the glens of Iveleary,
> And beloved Gougane Barra is all covered with clouds.

It is evident from this song that some of Mary O'Leary's family were on the run:

> I feel for your father and mother without you,
> For your bedmate and child crying out for you.
> The reason why I had not come to see you:
> I was every morning on the watch for my dear ones.

The Englishman, Smith, was buried for a few days in Tooreenduff, exhumed in the night by the Rockites, and dumped into the bog at Gortnalloughra, at a place that became known locally as Smith's Hole. The body was later removed to the Church of Ireland graveyard at Inchigeelagh, and a slab placed on the grave courtesy of James Barry, the unpopular landlord who built his mansion next to the old O'Leary tower house, Carrignaneelagh Castle. This is the inscription:

> Here rest the remains of John Smith, late of the 39th Reg.
> Aged 32 years. This stone was erected to his memory by
> Major Logan's Comp. 23rd Batt. Rifle Brigade in testimony
> of the high esteem they hold the 39th Reg. AD 1822.

Rockite Séamus Walsh was on the run for five years after the battle. When finally brought to justice, he was not executed like some of the others. Two members of the Muskerry militia, John Warren and Capt. Hedges, intervened and Walsh was pardoned. Two of Mary O'Leary's sons were also captured and charged with Smith's murder. However, they were released because of an effective defence by Daniel O'Connell, the lawyer and statesman instrumental in securing the passing of the Catholic Emancipation Act in 1829. O'Connell's family connection with the O'Learys probably explains his agreement to defend Mary O'Leary's sons. His aunt was Eibhlín Dhubh Ní Chomhnaill (Dark-haired Eileen O'Connell), widow of the famous Munster folk hero Art O'Leary. Mary O'Leary composed a poem for Daniel O'Connell in gratitude for saving her sons.

The Battle of Keimaneigh, not least because of Mary O'Leary's poem, became the most significant event in the local history of the area. Every event that occurred beforehand or afterwards was dated locally from the year of the battle.

When the tithe laws were repealed, the militia units were disbanded and peace returned to the area. In her poetry, Mary O'Leary turned her mind to other public concerns, keeping the spirit of Gaelic pride alive in the hearts of her people. Here are some lines from the song entitled *A Mháire ní Laoghaire* ("Oh Mary O'Leary"), in which she expresses her feelings about those who would embrace the language of the invader:

> I have heard some news for you now of late
> From the golden plover in Doughill
> That a time would be set at once in Erin
> When the bears would all be routed
> That the Repealers would arrive in full array
> And with God's aid to steer them
> Leave English speakers wineless and feastless
> With a volley of bullets to wake them.

In 1998, the Bantry and Ballingeary historical societies installed a monument in the Pass of Keimaneigh, on land donated by Pat Twomey of Bantry, to commemorate the 1822 battle. The bronze plaque, attached to an irregular-shaped slab of sandstone, mined from a local quarry, is inscribed in Irish and English as follows:

I gcuimhne na bhfear a cailleadh   To commemorate those who died

---

[28] This line, not translated on the English plaque, says that Edward Ring was hanged in March 1822.

I Gcath Chéim an Fhia
In Eanair na bliana 1822.
Mícheál Ó'Cathasaigh, Barra
Ó'Laoire,
Amhlaoibh Ó'Loinsigh.
(Buachaillí Bána Áitiúla)
Seán Mac Gabhann (Fórsaí na
nGall)
Crocadh Éamonn Ó'Rinn i Márta
1822.[28]
Ar dheis Dé go raibh a n-
anamacha.

At and after the Battle of
Keimaneigh
January 1822.
Michael Casey, Barry O'Leary,
Auliffe Lynch, Edward Ring[29]
(Local Whiteboys)
John Smith (Crown Forces)
May they rest in peace.

Another monument in the Pass, a marble and stone memorial erected in 1977, stands in tribute to Mary O'Leary herself. On the façade, in Irish, are inscribed the words:

To the east of this monument
The Whiteboys of Iveleary
Did battle with the yeomen
In the year 1822, during the tithe war.
Mary O'Leary
1774-1848
A poet who was born in Tooreennanean
And lived at the Inches
Celebrated the occasion with the famous song
The Battle of Keimaneigh
'Praise be to Jesus
That we didn't regret the attack
But commemorate the occasion with joy.'
This monument was erected by the people
Of this district to memorialize the event
On the 150th anniversary of the battle.

---

[29] Also known as William Ring.

MARY O'LEARY AND HER POEMS

Mary O'Leary was one of the last of the true Gaelic bards. Although the nineteenth century was a period of severe disruption and decline for the Irish-speaking population, there were a number of industrious souls, farmers, clergy and schoolteachers, who devoted what energy they could in adverse times to cultivating and preserving their language and literary traditions.

The penal laws, which punished the Irish for celebrating their language and heritage, produced a devastating effect on the Irish literary arts. Daniel Corkery, author of *The Hidden Ireland*, refers to the situation at the beginning of the 1800s:

> The Bardic Schools have now been closed for almost two centuries, the Courts of Poetry meet no more. The Gaelic literary tradition is slowly making an end. A poet here and there arises, and, stirred by a local catastrophe — as Máire Ní Laoghaire (Mary O'Leary) by the agrarian troubles of 1822 in West Cork —strikes out a song of fire and vigour or, emulous of the men of old, writes patiently a few verses in bardic metre. But the literary tradition is no more, for it has lost the power to create new forms.[30]

Mary O'Leary, operating in the folk-poetry idiom, was one of the Munster poets who wrote the final chapter of the unbroken literary history of Gaelic Ireland before a specifically Irish literature in English began to emerge. She drew her inspiration from a Celtic tradition that was almost two millennia old when she was born. The ancient Celtic poets, *filí*, were esteemed members of the aristocracy who specialized in praising nobles and warriors, and were experts on genealogy. Many of them could trace their family roots back to the Flood.

The *filí* were known to be powerful satirists, capable of exposing even the mightiest kings to public ridicule. Mary O'Leary displayed

---

[30] *The Hidden Ireland: A Study of Gaelic Munster in the Eighteenth Century* (Gill and Macmillan, 1924).

a similar talent for heaping scorn upon the high and mighty when she sang at the end of "The Battle of Keimaneigh":

> I'll sing no more, I've grown too old.
> I'm full of spite for those big-bellied porks.
> I've no more to say, I don't like their way,
> Raided and routed may that be their store.

Mary O'Leary composed alone and in conjunction with Denis Lynch of Ballyvourney. During the early part of the twentieth century, two folklore collectors from West Cork — Donal Lucey and Conor A. Cotter — gathered and transcribed several of her poems and noted that some of them were collaborations. On the manuscript of *A Mháire ní Laoghaire*, for example, Lucey noted that "Mary Burke, Keimaneigh, composed seven verses of this song, and Denis Lynch, Ballyvourney, composed the first and last verses." These transcripts are now housed in the Boole Library at University College Cork.

No sketches or paintings of Mary O'Leary have ever been found. The only physical description available comes from biographer Fr. Donncha Ó Donnchú who, based on interviews with her grandchildren, described her as a "strong, dark-haired woman, fairly tall, and of sallow complexion" — a characteristic which seems to have led to some criticism from those who knew her. But, as Ó Donnchú added, her complexion was part of her inheritance: "If it were a sin to be sallow, then thousands are damned."

Though better off than many of her poorer neighbours, Mary O'Leary empathized with their situation because she had known poverty in her youth. She also understood the extent to which their spirit had been shattered after years of oppression. There never could be a full-scale peasant revolt in Ireland, Mary O'Leary believed. Any rebellion would have to be launched with outside help.

Mary O'Leary and the other Munster poets of that era have been sometimes condemned by nationalist historians for allegedly undermining whatever spirit of independence the Irish might have possessed at that time, when she encouraged them to look for outside help rather than take matters into their own hands. Her poem, "The Battle of Keimaneigh," offers a characteristic example:

> Many men will fast approach using a ship of vast proportion,

And the French, down south, who are so stoic are ready for
the fray.
Cities will be razed, fires will be flamed,
Payment is due, the reckoning has come.

Likewise, in the poem "The Dawning of the Day" she says:

For I have to go down to Lower Clair Luirc with my news,
To see the French fleet under full sail.

Mary O'Leary was not being unpatriotic, however, when she
urged her countrymen to look to France for their salvation. She and
her fellow poets were merely describing the situation as they saw it.
The Irish, they believed, did not have the means or the ability to
carry this struggle through to a satisfactory conclusion. In her song
"On a Sunny Hillside," which is a classic aisling or vision poem,
Mary O'Leary tells of a poet dreaming about a beautiful maiden. He
asks her various questions before deciding she is, in fact, Ireland, the
Dark Rosaleen herself. The maid tells the poet she has been
imprisoned, then left needy and cold. But her day of freedom from
captivity is at hand. When the French arrive, she will be liberated:

To greet her I came with the aim that I might her beguile
Hoping further to share in her favours and win her bright
smile:
"Come with me today and stay to rest for awhile
In a feather-bed safe, if you care, for a month at a time."

"Don't mock me, my dear," said she, "I've not come to play.
I don't know your people or the street or home where you
stay
But I must with speed get to reach all of Ireland today
To tell them the Fleet is in Whiddy with all its array."

As a female, Mary O'Leary was part of another honourable
tradition. Early Irish poetry is said to be the only literature in Europe,
and perhaps in the world, where one finds a succession of women
poets. Why did poetry always seem a natural mode of expression for

gifted Irish women? Writer John Montague believes it was because of the lack of discrimination against them.[31]

The first female poet in recorded Irish literary history, Liadan of Corcaguiney, was a fully qualified member of the poets' guild, which meant she would have studied for up to 12 years. It was as an equal that the poet Curithir wooed her, and though she drove him off — for religious reasons — her lament rings across the centuries.

There is a long line of funereal laments in the history of Irish literature. One of the most famous is the majestic *Lament for Art O'Leary*, composed by his widow Eibhlín Dhubh Ní Chomhnaill (Dark-haired Eileen O'Connell), which survived long enough in the folk tradition to have been written down by nineteenth century collectors. How accurately it was preserved, however, remains a matter of conjecture.

Mary O'Leary's oral funerary songs include a lament for the executed Rockite William Ring, and a dirge for her son John Burke, also a member of the Rockites and apparently also executed. In the poem to her son, composed on behalf of his widow, she expresses a wide range and depth of emotion:

> Stay away from him, you green-coloured hawkmoths.[32]
> Do not tread on the grave of my brave hero.
> For he is my lover and my bedmate
> and my first wedded husband since I was a child.

Other themes in Mary O'Leary's folk poetry include devotion to Ireland expressed as part of a religious vision of the universe, stories of anguish and sorrow, songs of fun and love, and drinking refrains of joy and rowdyism. Daily life, even among the poorer class of Irish tenants and agricultural laborers, was not bereft of joys. Holidays, fairs, and even wakes were festive occasions, spiced with music, dancing, and the inevitable *uisce beatha* (water of life, i.e. whiskey). There was always hope, as Mary O'Leary said in *Tá Gaedhil Bhocht Cráidthe* ("The Poor Gaels Are In Torment") for a better tomorrow:

---

[31] Cf. *The Faber Book of Irish Verse*, edited by John Montague (Faber and Faber, 1974).

[32] The elephant hawkmoth, "found in dark places and regarded with aversion. On being discovered, it is instantly killed, as it is believed to sting cattle severely in the muzzle." (An Irish-English Dictionary by Rev. Patrick S. Dinneen, MA, Irish Texts Society, 1927).

When we defeat them, let none of you squabble about
a pint or a quart to put on the score.
But barrels, full tall ones, brought in and piled in the hallway
will supply thousands of callers with gallons galore.

But before those barrels of stout could be consumed, as she also declares in "The Poor Gaels Are In Torment," the enemy would have to be overthrown:

May scourge and wounding and terror consuming
befall that group in the midst of their store.
The hangman with rope wrapped around their throats,
and the Lord withholding his eyes from their plight.
And in place of our youth left there to languish
May that group be in anguish till Doomsday comes.

The destiny of her native country was linked inextricably in Mary O'Leary's mind to the will of God. Whatever way the people of Ireland went, God went with them. In the midst of all their troubles, their hopes for something better remained undimmed, their faith and trust in God remained strong. Her religious vision is expressed in such lines as:

I have heard from the prophets what Saint John has told us,
That the time of withholding has drawn to a close.
That ripe for the slaughter are those big-bellied butchers
Who have rejected Christ's Passion for orgies and sport.

Toward the end of "The Battle of Keimaneigh" her natural instinct is to give thanks:

Praise to the Lord Jesus, no reprisals have we known.[33]
And can speak of it gleefully, secure in our home."

Her love songs express themes of hope and longing, as well as the kind of practical advice she offers to a young woman in the song, *Bearta Crua* ("Hard Plight"):

---

[33] Her reference to the lack of reprisals would indicate that Mary O'Leary composed the song before the hanging of William Ring and other participants in the battle.

My stately maiden, there will be many a promise,
False and baseless made to your face.
But without the clergy's binding, don't yield to any man.
And you will gain the prize like Una,[34] if he should promise
you Ireland.
Every sod of it to be yours, without dispute or squabble.
Take my advice, do not believe the rake.
With such as him, avoid all intimacy.

In her song, *Fáinne an Lae* ("The Dawning of the Day"), she says:

Oh pleasing maid of form more fair than snow on a sunny
hill,
You have left me sick and sore with little rest from pain.
I would marry you without a farthing, and I would not ask
for cows or dowry.
But I am already vowed to a pretty young woman of this
neighbourhood, though it be against my will.

Biographer Ó Donnchú notes cryptically that none of Mary
O'Leary's descendants inherited her poetic talent. As a local sage is
reputed to have remarked at the time, "When the woman's poetry
stops, that will be the end of it."

That was not the end of it, however. If the fires of nationalism and
devotion to the Roman Catholic faith still burn strongly in the hearts
of the people who live in the Irish-speaking area of West Cork, it is
due in no small part to the enduring contribution of Mary O'Leary.
As the poet of her people, she was always there to counsel and
encourage her neighbours. Her songs were sung at fairs, at social
events, and by the fireside. If the native language — no longer
spoken by the bulk of the Irish population — is still flourishing in
this region, if the old songs are still being sung, and the stories are
still being retold, the people have Mary O'Leary to thank for her
efforts in preserving and sustaining that heritage. She celebrated it in
song, and left a remarkable legacy. My goal, in writing this little
book, has been to bring her achievement to the attention of a wider
audience.

---

[34] Una — the banshee (fairy woman) of the O'Carroll clan.

THE SONGS OF MARY O'LEARY[35]

<hr />

[35] Because they have undergone a triple process of appropriation, these versions of Mary O'Leary's songs, translated by Fr. Seán Sweeney, SMA, can offer little more than the flavour of the originals. The songs were never written down during her lifetime, or even immediately afterwards, but passed orally from generation to generation, and thus became vulnerable to all the alterations and errors that can occur through this process. The Irish versions of these songs were collected around the turn of the twentieth century by two folklorists from West Cork, Donal Lucey and Conor A. Cotter. These pioneers in the revival of the Irish language transcribed the poems phonetically and compiled them into manuscripts that are now housed in the archives of the Boole Library at University College Cork. The majority of the translated songs in this section come from that source. Other songs were collected by biographer Ó Donnchú from Jeremiah A. Cotter, Conor O'Moynihan and Michael (Sheahan) Hyde. They are presented more or less chronologically, using much of the same Old Irish spelling with attendant spelling inconsistencies that Fr. Ó Donnchú employed in the 1930s.

AR LEACAIN NA GRÉINE

I

Ar leacain na gréine inné is mé ag múscailt mo bhó 'sea dhearcas-sa
lem thaobh an spéirbhean mhómhail mhúinte dheas óg.
Do bhí lasa na gcaor 'na gné agus a gnúis mar an rós,
Agus a cúl carnfholt péarlach léi go dúnaibh a bróga.

II

Níor dhanaid liom féin teacht faoi n-a deimhin le n-a fáilte is le n-a
póg,
Ach are eagla nárbh aon bhean tsaolta a thárlaigh im threo.
Níorbh aithnid liom féin dá mhéid é a trácht insa chóig —
Ach a pearsa agus a méinn a scéimh, a cáil, is a cló.

III

Is 'na haice siúd do shíos is do luíos ar phlámaireacht léi.
Agus, is gairid arís, gur shaoileas bheith páirteach seal léi:
"Má taoi tuirseach ón tslí dein mhoill is go lá tar liom féin.
Is ghabhair leaba — nach tuí — ar feadh mí má's áil leat gabháil léi."

IV

"Tá magadh ort, a mhaoin," adúirt sí, "Is ní hábhar duit mé,
Agus ná feadar cá luíonn do thíos ná t'áitreabh féin.
Mar caithfidh dul síos go híochtar Clár Luirc lem scéal.
Go bheaca-sa an Fleet i bhFaoide, 'na lánchumas tréan."

ON A SUNNY HILLSIDE[36]

I

On a sunny hillside yesterday, as I was waking my cows,
A fair lady I saw, modest, well-mannered, comely and young.
The blush of berries was on her face, and her countenance like the rose,
And her abundant tresses flowed down to the clasps of her shoes.

II

I would gladly have come over to her to welcome her with a kiss,
But I feared she might be some ethereal woman who had happened my way.
I did not recognize her despite all that was said in the province[37] about her —
Her person, her visage, her beauty, her fame and her form.

III

I sat down beside her and started to flatter her.
And, again soon after, I thought of sharing friendship with her:
"If you're tired from travelling, stop off and come with me for the day.
And you'll get a bed — not a straw one — for a month, if you wish it that way."

IV

"You are jesting, my dear," said she. "And you have no cause to do so with me,
Seeing that I do not know where lies your home or your habitation.
For I must go to the North of Lorc's Plain[38] with the news
That I have seen the Fleet[39] in Whiddy,[40] equipped in full power."

---

[36] Composed around 1797. Collected by Fr. Ó Donnchú from Jeremiah A. Cotter of Currihy West.

[37] The province — Munster

[38] Clár Luirc — Lorc's Plain — poetic name for Ireland. Leary Lorc, son of Iugane the Great, high king of Ireland about 300 AD.

[39] The Fleet. On 14 December 1796, the French headed for Ireland with a great fleet. Gen. Lazare Hoche was in command, aboard the ship *La Fraternité*. A storm blew up, scattering the ships. Some sank and others drifted into Bantry Bay. Thus failed the Armada. The survivors sailed home on 28 December.

[40] Whiddy Island in Bantry Bay, near which some of the French arrived in 1796.

V

"A mhascalaigh mhín thar an bhFleet ná trácht liom go héag.
Mar is le hanacra do chím-se na mílte I ngátar 'na déidh.
Tháinig scaipeadh ortha ón ngaoi fóríor chuir a lán acu ar strae.
Agus I nglasaibh 'sea do shuíd mar an Rí-bhean seo thárlaigh i gcéin.

VI

"Gach duine acu chífir mínigh dóibh brí mo scéil.
Go bhfuilid ag tíocht go buínear faoi ghrán is faoi philéar.
Gearradh ghroí — an Laoiseach san Spáinneach— dá réir.
Go Banba ag tíocht gan mhoill le grásta Mhic Dé.

VII

"Go deimhin má's fíor do laoithe a stáidbhruinneal séimh,
Beidh talamh gan chíos, gan íoc, gan cháin, is gan pléi.
Beidh cruinneacht is im is saill ar an gclár againn féin.
Agus gasra an ghrinn ag díogadh na gcárt agus dá nglaoch."

V[41]

"My warrior sweet, of the Fleet do not talk to me any more.
So distressful to me is the grief it has brough to our shore.
The winds blew so fiercely over the deep that it sent many of them astray.
So now in shackles they sit, as happened to the regal lady[42] long ago."

VI

"To each one that you see, give the news that they are coming.
They are coming in force with powder and bullets and gun.
Stout-hearted supporters hastening — Louis[43] and the Spaniard[44] — as one.
To Banba's[45] green shore they are coming, without delay, by the grace of God's son.

VII

"Indeed, if your descriptions are true, my stately, gentle maiden,
We shall have land without rent, without tax or dispute.
We shall have wheat and butter and salted meat on the table for ourselves.
And merrymakers will be draining the quarts, and calling for more."

---

[41] Fr. Ó Donnchú suggests that this verse, dealing with the aftermath of the Armada, belongs to another song because it seems out of place in this context.

[42] Regal lady — the Queen of England, possibly Anne Boleyn, the executed second wife of Henry VIII.

[43] Louis — Louis XVI of France. His name is intended to signify military aid from France.

[44] The Spaniard — indicating the whole nation of Spain. At that time, England was waging war against France, Spain and the Netherlands. Ireland would depend on military aid from these countries if it were to wage war with England.

[45] Poetic name for Ireland.

Fáinne an Lae — (1)

I

Maidean moch is mé i bhfeidhil mo stuic agus dá seola chun an fhéir
'Sea bhuail umam 's í stuaire an tsuilt is í ag duanaireacht is ag
éigheamh.
Nuair a chuala an guth ba chuairce liom, le fonn gur dhruideas léi.
Ba raimhre gach deoir le n-a leacain bhuig. Agus ba thrua í,
ag gol i gcéin.

II

Ba chrothach, scuabach, dualach tiú a cuacha ag tuitim léi.
A com seang singil ba néata suíte is a mala dheas ba chaol.
A déidh ba ghile is a béal ba bhinne is a dá cích chruinne ghéar.
"Go deimhin, a bhean ba bhreá, do ghean go moch le fáinne an lae."

III

"An tú Céarnait ghlic an bhé cheap muileann amach a t'intinn ghéar?
Nó an Bhé a thuga thar barr na toinne do mhúscail Cath na Trae?
Nó an fíor gur tú thug an t-úill so b'fhinne thar mhná na chruinne léi?
Nárbh áluinn deas é a scéimh 'sa gean
Go moch le fáinne an lae?"

THE DAWNING OF THE DAY — (1)[46]

I

'Twas early morning as I was tending my stock and driving them out to pasture
That I encountered the stately maiden of mirth crooning and crying.
When I heard the voice so pleasing to me, I eagerly drew close to her.
The largest tears were on her soft cheeks.
And how pitiful she was, weeping so far from home.

II

Wavy, flowing, thickly ringleted, were her tresses falling down.
Trimly set was her slender waist, and her eyebrows neat and fine.
With brightest teeth and sweetest lips and her two breasts, round, upright.
"Indeed, oh woman grand would be your love in the early dawning day."

III

"Are you the clever Cearnet[47] who shaped the mill out of her acute mind?
Or, are you the Lady[48] brought over the waves who sparked the Battle of Troy?
Or, is it true that you are the one who won that most precious apple
Over all the women in the world?
How lovely and sweet are her looks and her love in the early dawning day.

---

[46] Collected by Donal Lucey, this song seems to have been composed a few years before the Rising of 1798, an unsuccessful series of rebellions staged under the auspices of Wolfe Tone's United Irishmen. The Rising is usually considered one of the great milestones of Irish history, giving rise to the birth of modern Irish nationalism.

[47] Cearnet — the beautiful daughter of a Pictish king of Scotland. She was loved by King Cormac MacArt of Ireland. Cormac's wife, Ethni Ollamda, compelled the girl to grind nine pecks of grain every day on a hand-mill. Bearing Cormac's child, and unable to work at milling, she appealed to the King who immediately sent to Scotland for men to construct a mill, thus relieving her from drudgery.

[48] Lady — Helen of Troy, she whose face sank a thousand ships.

IV

"A sháirfhir ghlic na ráite suilt ní haoinne 'ca-san mé.

Ach bé is ea mé gan chéile ar bith cé gur fada mé faoi lean.

Beir scéal anois gur daoragh sinn ag tréatha an oilc 'san chluain.

Gan bhréag anois tá an téarma istigh beidh Éire againn faoi réim."

V

"Dá mb'áil leat teacht ti'n tábhairne isteach is bheith páirteach seal liom féin?"

'Sé an freagra adúirt: "Níl caoi dhom stad tá an fómhar ar leatha im dhéidh.

An Diúc a York 'sa thrúp dá shlad ag priúnsa ceart na nGael.

'S ar an mbliain seo chughainn beidh búir go lag.

"Sin cúntas ceart lem scéal."

IV

"Oh clever hero of merry words, I am not any one of those.
I am a maid without spouse, though long have I been in anguish.
Bear then the news that I was enslaved by wicked, perverse hordes.
But now, in truth, the time has come, we will have Erin in full sway."

V

"Would you like to come into this inn
and share friendship with me for a while?
The answer she gave: 'I cannot stop, for it is Harvest Day.
The Duke of York[49] and his troops are being ravaged
by the true Prince of the Gael.
And in one year more the boors will lie prostrate.
"That is the true account of my tidings."

---

[49] The Duke of York — leader of the English in the war against France in 1793.

FÁINNE AN LAE — (2)

I
Maidean moch ar leaba bhuig do chuala guth na n-éin.
Do smaoineas-sa gur chór dom dul ag múscailt stuic chun féir.
Do bhuail umam is a ciabh 'na hucht, is í ag cíora a foilt go réi.
An chúileann ghlic ba bhreátha cruth ná an eala ar tsruth an éisc.

II
Mo chroí gur chrith 'á fhiafraí de cad é an tír gurbh as an bhé:
"An tú péarla an tsuilt ón nGréig do rith agus d'fhág 'na raic an
Trae?
Nó Déirdre thug grá cléibh is cion do Naoise a cailleadh léi?
Nó an bhean a rug le háilleacht cruth an t-úll ó iomaí ghéar?

THE DAWNING OF THE DAY — (2)[50]

I

One early morning as I lay on my soft bed, I heard the voices of the birds.
I thought to myself that I should go and let out the stock to graze.
I met her then, her tresses on her lap, as she gently combed her hair:
The gifted maiden of form more fair than the swan on fish-abounding stream.

II

My heart quaked as I asked her what country the lady was from:
"Are you the pearl of mirth who fled from Greece, and left Troy in ruins?
Or Deirdre[51] who gave heart's love and affection to Naoise,[52] who died because of her?
Or the woman who, by the beauty of her form, won the apple[53] in keen competition?

---

[50] A version of the poem collected by Cornelius O'Moynihan of Kilkenny.
[51] Deirdre — In Irish mythology, she was the foster-child of Conor MacNeasa, king of Ultonia (Ulster).
[52] Naoise — In Irish mythology, he was the husband of Deirdre. Both were principals in a tale of love of treachery set in the time of the Red Branch Knights of Ulster.
[53] Venus, Juno and Minerva were three beautiful goddesses, caught in a dilemma because nobody could determine who was the most beautiful. This caused friction between them, and they took the case to court. Paris was the judge. He decided that a golden apple should be awarded to the one judged most beautiful. Venus won the apple.

III

"An tú Clíona ghlic chuir draoícht is broid? Nó Aoibhill dheas gan
claon?
Nó stuaire an tuir do ghluais thar muir, agus d'fhág na mílte tréith?
Nó an bhean sa chnoc do thraoch na coin go nglaoís Cuileann
tséimh?
Chuir Fionn 'sa tsruth gan chrích gan choin d'fhúig deorach fliuch an
Fhéinn?"

IV

Do labhair sí liom: "A chéimhfhir, suí go n-ínnsead fá mo scéil.
Ní stuaire mé do ghluais thar muir ná mhúscail Cath na Trae,
De natives chirt Uíbh Laoghaire mé is de shíolra mhaithe Gael.
Is mo chómhra dein mara bpósfair mé go moch le fáinne an lae."

V

A bháb an tsuilt is breátha cruth 'na sneachta ar chnoc le gréin,
Is d'fhágais-se tinn breoite mé is ní mór mo shos ó phéin.
Do phósfainn-se gan feoirling tú is ní iarrainn ba ná spré.
Ach tá móid orm le hógbhean dheis don chomharsanacht roim ré."

III

"Are you the clever Cleena[54] who wrought bewitchment and distress?
Or the lovely Aoibhill[55] without deceit?
Or the fair maid of the tower who crossed over the sea, and left
thousands in feeble state?
Or the woman on the hill who subdued the hounds, the one called
Cuileann the Mild?
And put Fionn[56] in the stream in helpless plight, and left the Fianna[57]
in tears?"

IV

She said to me: "Kind sir, sit down till I explain my situation.
I am not the maid who rode over the sea or sparked the Battle of
Troy,
but a true born native of Iveleary of noble Gaelic lineage.
And my coffin make, if I am not wed by early dawning day."

V

Oh pleasing maid of form more fair than snow on a sunny hill,
You have left me sick and sore with little rest from pain.
I would marry you without a farthing, and I would not ask for cows
or dowry.
But I am already vowed to a pretty young woman of this
neighbourhood, though it be against my will."

---

[54] Cleena — a famous Munster goddess of ancient Irish lore. Queen of the
Munster fairy host, she is said to dwell at Carrigcleena (Cleena's rock) near
Mallow, County Cork. Tonn Cliodna (Glandore Bay) is named after her
because she is believed to have drowned there after coming there with her
husband, the earthly Ciabhan Mac Eachach.
[55] Aoibhill — another goddess of ancient Irish lore. A fairy woman of the
Dalcassians, she is said to live in North Munster.
[56] Fionn Mac Cool — the legendary Irish warrior hero.
[57] Fianna — Fionn Mac Cool's band of warriors.

BEARTA CRUA

I

Tráth go déannach a ghabhas liom féinig trasna chaoltha ar dhrúcht dom,

Bhí lonnradh ó Phoébus gan smúit gan éclips ag teacht go réighlan chughainn-ne.

Bhí cantain éanlaith ar bharraibh géaga,

Is ar linn bhí éisc 'á múscailt,

Nuair a dhearcas taobh liom an chúileann mhaorga chuir saighead trím thaobh le Cúpid.

II

"Ghabhair machaí lán' uaim do bhuaidh le háireamh gan chíos, gan cháin ag glaoch ort,

An cupa, an pláta go rithfá rás leo

Is a dtabhairt id láimh gan bhaochas.

Do ghabhair an fháinne thug Fionn sa tsnáimh leis chun bheith

Gach lá ar do mhéaraibh.

Luinneog: Is ghabhaidh tú, a uainí, gach ní dá ndúirt leat

Ach na bearta crua so réite.

III

"Is ghabhaidh tú, a mhaoiní, an tsleagh chinn faobhair

Bhí ag Aicil chúineach éachtach.

Le barra púinte do threascair

Faoinlag Hector groí 'sa Trae thoir.

An bhratuinn shíoda a bhí casta timpeall ag teacht thar tuinn ar Hélen. S

Luinneog: Is ghabhaidh tú, a uainí, gach ní dá ndúirt leat

Ach na bearta crua so réite.

HARD PLIGHT[58]

I

One evening late as I went alone across the dewy narrows,
The radiance from Phoebus,[59] without cloud or eclipse, was softly
approaching me.
There was chanting of birds on the tops of the branches,
And in the pool the fish were stirring,
When I saw beside me the stately maid who pierced my side with
Cupid's[60] arrow

II

"You'll have from me full fields of cattle to count, with no tax or rent
demanded,
The cup and plate you could run a race with, held in your hand so
easily.
You'll get the ring that Fionn took into the water with him
To be each day on your finger.
Refrain: And you'll receive, my dear, all I have promised
If you solve my hard plight for me.

III

"And you'll get, my dear, the sharp-edged spear
Held once by the famed and mighty Achilles.[61]
With the point of which he laid out low the great Hector over in
Troy.
The silken pennon that was wrapped around Helen as she crossed
over the sea
Refrain: And you'll receive, my dear, all I have promised
If you solve my hard plight for me.

---

[58] Collected by Donal Lucey. There seem to be stanzas missing between I
and II. The repeated refrain suggests that Mary O'Leary wanted an audience
to join in the chorus.
[59] Phoebus — a name given to Apollo, son of Jupiter and Latrona. He was
often called the sun-god.
[60] Cupid — son of Venus.
[61] Achilles — the bravest hero of the Greeks in the battle of Troy. Killed
Hector, the most valiant hero of the other side.

IV

"Do ghabhair, a stóraí, na luana cródha
Bhí i ndaingean cheo 'sa Léin Loch,
Is an claíomh chinn ór nár gheallas fós duit
Thug Tailc Mhac Treóin go hÉirinn,
Dóbhair an t-úill uaim do pléi idir thriúr ban is bhua sa chúirt le
Vénus
Luinneog: Is ghabhaidh tú, a uainí, gach ní dá ndúirt leat
Ach na bearta crua so réite.

V

"Do ghabhair, a stóraí, an práisléad órdha do tharraig geoin is
éirleach
I gcaitheamh chomhraic 'sa bhFrainc ag Bóna is ag Laoiseach mór
gur traocha,
Do chuaidh faoi seol insa Spáinn le fórsa is d'fhág ag feocha céad
fear.
Luinneog: Is ghabhaidh tú, a uainí, gach ní dá ndúirt leat
Ach na bearta crua so réite.

VI

"Ghabhair an cochall draoíchta bhí ag an tsíbhean gurbh ainm
Clíona.
An réilthean a thug le díorais d'á chéile caoine
Is do cheil a ghnaoi ar na céadthaibh.
Do ghabhair an Fleece uaim — is ní ná hinnsim —
Thug Jason 'na luing don Ghréig leis,
Luinneog: Is ghabhaidh tú, a uainí, gach ní dá ndúirt leat
Ach na bearta crua so réite.

IV

"And you'll get, my love, the valorous blades[62]
That were kept in the misty dungeon of Lough Lein.
And the gold-topped sword which I had not yet promised you
Brought by Talc Mac Treoin to Ireland.
You'll receive from me the apple the three women disputed about
Which was won at court by Venus.
Refrain: And you'll receive, my dear, all I have promised
If you solve my hard plight for me.

V

"You'll get, my love, the golden bracelet that brought about tumult and havoc
In the conflict in France with Bonaparte which was subdued by Louis the Great,
And who sailed into Spain with armed forces, leaving a hundred men to perish.
Refrain: And you'll receive, my dear, all I have promised
If you solve my hard plight for me.

VI

"You'll get the magic hood of the fairy woman whose name was Cleena.
The fair one who gave it with love to her kindly spouse,
Whose good looks she concealed from hundreds.
You'll get from me the Fleece — which I don't tell of —
That Jason took aboard from Greece with him.
Refrain: And you'll receive, my dear, all I have promised
If you solve my hard plight for me.

---

[62] Blades — swords.

VII

"Is ghabhair an bhó uaim a bhí i Beótia is Argus mór 'á haoireacht.
Do bhí aici clover is togha na córach do thuit le ceol Orpheus.
Ghabhair Bran is Sceolang a leaga lóthairt,
Is dheine spórt don Fhéinn seal.
Luinneog: Is ghabhaidh tú, a uainí, gach ní dá ndúirt leat
Ach na bearta crua so réite.

VIII

"Ghabhair capall Dhomhnaill, ná hiarrann feoise is ná hitheann lón
ná béile.
Is tréan la fórsa do bhuaile bóthar faoi scamall cheo sa Léin Loch.
An londubh ceolmhar ón gCarn Chrón uaim is athach mór na gcaora.
Luinneog: Is ghabhaidh tú, a uaní, gach ní dá ndúirt leat
Ach na bearta crua so réite."

IX

A chúileann mhaorga is mó geallamhaint bhréagach,
'Á thabhairt 'od bhéal gan bhunús duit.
Is gan ceangal cléire le fear ná claonaigh.
Is ghabhair an chraobh mar Úna,
Dá ngeallfadh Éire.
'Na fódaibh caola is í thabhairt gan phléi gan siúit duit.
Mo chomhairle déin-se is ná creid an réice is le fear dá chéird na
cionntaigh.

VII

"You'll get from me the Beotian cow,[63] guarded by the great Argus.[64]
She had clover and excellent provisions but succumbed to the music
of Orpheus.[65]
You'll have Bran and Sceolang[66] that brought down so much game,
And often made sport for the Fianna.
Refrain: And you'll receive, my dear, all I have promised
If you solve my hard plight for me.

VIII

"You'll get Donal's horse, which never needs rest or eats any food or
meal.
He would speedily on the road set out under a cloud of mist to Lough
Lein.
You'll get the singing blackbird from Carnacrone and the great giant
of the sheep.
Refrain: And you'll receive, my dear, all I have promised
If you solve my hard plight for me."

IX

My stately maiden, there will be many a promise,
False and baseless made to your face.
But without the clergy's binding, don't yield to any man.
And you will gain the prize like Una,[67] if he should promise you
Ireland.
Every sod of it to be yours, without dispute or squabble.
Take my advice, do not believe the rake.
With such as him, avoid all intimacy.

---

[63] Beotian cow — Juno gave it to Argus to watch over. Minerva put Argus's
one hundred eyes to sleep and killed him.
[64] Argus — son of Avestor — a huge giant with one hundred eyes.
[65] Mary O'Leary suggests here that Orpheus put Argus to sleep with his
music. In fact, it was Minerva who did it.
[66] Bran and Sceolang — the hounds of Fionn Mac Cool.
[67] Una — the banshee (fairy woman) of the O'Carroll clan.

SEÓ LEÓ, A THOIL

I

Mo ghraidhin go breá tú, a pháistín óg
Mar taoin tú buartha suaite dreoil.
Má thíonn tú liom-sa ghabhair fothain is coir.
Agus ghabhaidh tú duais nár lua leat fós.
Agus seó leó, a thoil, as ná goil go fóil.

II

Do ghabhair chun bainne uaim macha breá bó.
Agus ghabhaidh tú an tarbh chun clasaithe leo.
Ghabhair na capaill chun branair is rómhair,
Agus do ghabhair fíon dearg is a mhalairt ar bórd.
Agus seó leó, a thoil, as ná goil go fóil.

III

Ghabhair an clogad san sciath ón Amadán Mór.
Agus ghabhaidh tú an t-úll ón gcúilfhinn óg.
Ghabhair an gadhar ba mheidhrighe seol,
Do cheangail an laoch a héill 'na dheoidh.
Agus seó leó, a thoil, as ná goil go fóil.

IV

Ghabhair an corn faoi dheochanna sóil
Do chuire an draoícht ar na mílte sló.
Do ghabhair an chathair úd Dhún an Ór,
A bhí ag an nGrua Mór chun sport.
Agus seó leó, a thoil, as ná goil go fóil.

V

Ghabhair an lomra do foilce le hór,
Thug Jason 'na luing thar tuinn ar bórd.
Ghabhair na capaill faoi bhratannaibh sróll
Ó mhac rí an Deirg — cé gur fada dhó id choir.
Agus seó leó, a thoil, as ná goil go fóil.

So Hush, My Love[68]

I

God love you forever, my little lad, you are worried and weary and worn.
If you come with me, you'll find shelter and caring.
And you'll get a prize you haven't yet heard of.
So hush, my love, and cry no more

II

You will get from me a fine herd of cows to provide you with milk.
And also the bull to charm them.
You'll get horses to plough the grassland,
And red wine and white on your table.
So hush, my love, and cry no more

III

You'll get the helmet and the shield from the Great Fool.[69]
And the apple from the fair young lady.[70]
You'll get the dog of liveliest motion
Which the hero held in leash behind him.
So hush, my love, and cry no more

IV

You'll get the horn with delicious drinks that used to bewitch the thousands.
You'll get that mansion of Dún an Ór,[71] which the Great Ogre used for his pleasure.
So hush, my love, and cry no more.

V

You'll get the Fleece that was bathed in gold,
That Jason took aboard ship over the sea.
You'll get the horses draped in satin
From the son of King Derg — long meant for you.
So hush, my love, and cry no more

---

[68] Collected by Donal Lucey
[69] Great Fool — A fairy trickster who chooses his human victims randomly, disfiguring them with his touch.
[70] Fair young lady — Venus
[71] Dún an Ór — literally, the hill of gold, a mountain near Dingle, County Kerry.

VI

Ghabhair Mágh Chroma gan dabht chun bróg.
Agus gheofaí tú an Droichead chun "provision" lón.
Ghabhair Baile Átha Cliath chun fia is sport.
Agus ghabhair chun stuiceanna Luimneach mór.
Agus seó leó, a thoil, as ná goil go fóil.

VII

Gheofaí tú Béara chun éisc ar bórd.
Agus ghabhair an margadh leathan faoi fheoil.
Ghabhair na cuanta faoi bhádaibh seoil,
Agus ghabhair Uíbh Laoghaire chun sméar is cnó.
Agus seó leó, a thoil, as ná goil go fóil.

VIII

Ar an mbliain seo chughainn beidh búir faoi bhrón,
Is cathair is dún gan smúit gan cheo.
Do ghabhair-se ní nár mhaoís ort fós:
Is í iníon an Diúc id chlúid chun sport.
Agus seó leó, a thoil, as ná goil go fóil.

IX

Ná goil a thuille agus ná feicim do dheoir.
Mar beid siúd scriosta shar a dtigidh an fómhar.
Beidh a súile ag sile agus briste ar a nglór.
Is a gcóstí 'gainn-ne 'na ngliugaram sport.
Agus seó leó, a thoil, as ná goil go fóil.

VI

You'll be given Macroom, for sure, to provide you with shoes.
And the Drohid[72] by way of provision and food.
Dublin will be yours for hunting and sport.
And the great Limerick for your stock.
So hush, my love, and cry no more

VII

You'll get the Beara[73] to provide fish for your table.
And the wide marketplace for meat.
You'll have the harbours with their sailing boats,
And Iveleary for its berries and nuts.
So hush, my love, and cry no more.

VIII

By next year, the boors will be grieving,
And city and town cleared of smoke and fog.
You'll have a gift I haven't told you of yet:
The Duke's daughter in your chimney corner to amuse you.
So hush, my love, and cry no more.

IX

Don't cry any more, let me not see your tears.
For yonder crew will be wiped out before autumn comes.
Their eyes will be dripping and their voices will falter.
And we will have their coaches, to enjoy their jiggling and rattling.
So hush, my love, and cry no more.

---

[72] Drohid (Droichead) — the bridge. Perhaps Clondrohid, near Macroom.
[73] The Beara — the Hag of Beara, an ancient Celtic goddess who gave Irish kings the right to rule their lands.

AN BÚRCHACH

I

A Bhúrcaigh Óg ón gCéim, mar a dtéann an fia chun strae,
Fill thar n-ais, is beir leat bean
A dhéanfaidh beart dod réir.
Ná fág í siúd id dhéidh
Mar gheall ar bheagán spré.
Dá dtí a clan sa bhruín let ais,
Go mbuafaoi leat an sway.

II

Mara mbea crosa is fán an tsaol
Is bás a hathar féin,
Bhea flúirse mhór dá stoc annsúd
I ngaorthaíbh cúmhra ré.
Marcaíocht shocair shéimh
Is culaith dhen tsíoda dhaor,
Leaba chlúimh bhea faoi n-a cúm is cruitín dúnta léi.

III

'Sí Neil Ní Mhichíl Chnámhaigh
An eala mhúinte mhná,
Gaol na bhfear is na dtíosach gceart,
Thuill clú agus meas riamh d'fháil.
Seomraí brúchtaigh bhán
Is machaí bó ag tál.
Mná deáclúil 'na dtithe siúd
Do riarfa flúirse aráin.

YOUNG MAN OF THE BURKES[74]

I

Young man of the Burkes from Céim,[75] where the deer wander at will,
Return and bring back with you a woman who will be amenable to your wishes.
Do not leave that girl behind you because of a small dowry.
If her kin were at your side in a quarrel,[76] you would emerge victorious.

II

Were it not for life's misfortunes, and her father's death,
There would be stock in abundance there, on the rich, smooth meadowlands.
She would be riding at her ease in a suit of costly silk,
With a feather bed beneath her, and a curtain closed around her.

III

Big-boned Michael's daughter Nell is a well-mannered, swan-like maid,
Kin of upright, generous men, ever worthy of fame and respect.
Bright, well-furnished rooms are theirs, and herds of milking cows.
Famous are their household women for providing abundance of bread.

---

[74] Composed for one of Mary O'Leary's sons.
[75] Céim — Keimaneigh.
[76] Quarrel —Faction fighting was very common throughout the district in Mary O'Leary's times. On fair days and market days, and sometimes on Sunday evenings, the disturbances would break out. St. Finbarr's Day was noted for squabbles between factions from Kerry and Cork at Gougane Barra. In 1817, the Bishop of Cork halted the religious observances at Gougane because of the faction fighting.

IV

A Bhúrcaigh úd tá thua
Ag ciúmhais na Locha Lua,
Beidh ort an léan má thréigeann tusa
Craobhfholt dheas na gcuach.
Céile shocair shuairc
Do bhé dhis bhea gan ghruaim,
Go bhfuil an sway aici féin dá réir
Ó chaol an ghleanna go cuan.

V

Ar maidin Domhnaigh Dé
Is í thaistil chughainn thar Céim,
An ainnir mhúinte chneasta chlúiteach
Ba dheas é dlúth a dead.
Bhí lasadh lúr na gcaor
'Na leacain úir, bhuigh, réidh.
Ba phras é a siúl ar bharr an drúcht
Gur sciob sí an Búrchach léi.

IV

Oh young man of the Burkes, down there at the border of Lough
Lua,[77]
You will deeply regret it, if you abandon the maid of pretty tresses.
A quiet and pleasant wife she would be, this handsome, cheerful
maid,
Whose sway is rightly acknowledged from the foot of the glen to the
bay.

V

On God's own Sunday morning, she came toward us over the Céim,
The mild-mannered, gentle, well-known girl with the pretty, close-set
teeth.
The bright lustre of berries was on her fresh, soft, smooth cheeks.
Light was her step atop the dew, as she swept young Burke away.

---

[77] Lough Lua — a lake situated between the villages of Inchigeelagh and
Ballingeary. It is about 10 km long by 1 km wide.

TUAIREAMH SHEÁIN DE BÚRC

I

A Sheáin de Búrc, mo chúmha trím aeibh tú.
A bhuinneáin an chliatháin ghléigil,
Do chúm is gile ná feicim ag aon fhear.
Is go dtáinig go ró-mhoch ag fógairt an lae dhuit.

II

Ba bhinn do labhartha, banúil, béasach,
Is ba bhreá do phearsa 'na seasamh I n-aon bhall.
'Sis é mo léan ná déachas 'san uaigh leat.
Mh'uchlán, a bhuinneáin, do cheann ar an bhfuarma.

III

Tóg do cheann go 'n-neosad scéal duit,
Go bhfuilim gan fear, gan mhac, gan aoinne.
Tá an mathshlua mór so t'réis teacht at éileamh.
Ach éirí it seasamh is tabharfaigh siad saor tú.

IV

Mo thriúr deartháireacha, agus a ngearáin traochta.
Beirt ó Lonndain agus triúr ó Éirinn,
Páipéir bhreaca acu go daingean faoi séala.
Ag teacht led phárdún ón Rí saor chughat.

LAMENT FOR JOHN BURKE[78]

I

Oh, John Burke[79], my grief for you pierces my heart.
Oh fresh slender sprout of the lightsome body,
Whiter your waist than I have seen on any man.
And to think I have come too early to announce your day.

II

Sweet was your speech, modest, seemly,
Fine was your person, wherever you stood.
It is my anguish that I have not gone into the grave with you.
Alas, my sapling, your head is on the cold ground

III

Raise your head till I tell you of my plight,
That I am left without a husband or a son, or anyone.
This great congregation has come at your bidding.
Only rise to your feet, and they will free you.

IV

My three brothers have travelled, their horses are exhausted.
Two from London and the third from Ireland with writs duly sealed.
Bringing from the King a free pardon for you.

---

[78] Biographer Ó Donnchú included two versions of this lament because of the great differences between them. This version was collected by Donal Lucey.

[79] John Burke — Mary O'Leary's oldest son was said to be one of the Rockites captured and condemned to the gallows after the Battle of Keimaneigh. His wife's three brothers are said to have gone to England and obtained a pardon from the King, but failed to arrive back in time to save him from execution.

V

Mo chúig céad tuirse nach é Eilic do fága,
Nó Éamonn ó b'é an fear dob fhearr dhíobh,
Nó Toiríolach fionn geal, dalta mo mháthar,
Agus Seán de Búrc do theacht 'na shláinte.

VI

"Faire! Faire! A iníon ó, a Mháire,
Má taoin tú ar buile ná caill do náire.
Gurab usa dhuit feat fháil ná triúr deartháireacha.
Is céad moladh le Muire is iad mo leinbh a tháinig."

VII

Ní déarfása san go deimhin, a mháthair,
Dá mbeifá amuigh I n-Oileán an Tnáma,
Mar a bhfaghainn clóca greanta a bhea córithe ón Spáinn theas,
Agus culaithí ghabhagh barra ins gach aon áir go ngeoinn-se.

VIII

Láimhní dom ghlacaibh agus fáinní go leor uaigh,
Agus péarlaí le caitheamh nuair a thógfainn mar mheón é,
Buataisí greanta nár áirigheas-sa fós duit,
Is hataí ar mo bhathas chun aeridheachta 'gus spórt dom.

IX

Gabhainn plúr mín muilinn 'á rilleadh trí háirse,
Rósta milis agus imirt ar tháiplis,
Marcaíocht ar eachaibh groí stábla,
Agus cead codladh go cluthair idir a dhá láimh siúd.

X

Is beag an iongnadh mise go túirseach,
Mar is minic a chonnac tú ag doras do chúirte,
Mathshlua ar marcaíocht agus mathshlua ag túrlac
Agus na búird ar leathadh agus an solus gan múchadh.

V

My grief, five hundred fold that it wasn't Alec who was taken,
Or Éamonn, since he is the best of them,
Or fair-headed Terence, foster child of my mother,
And John Burke allowed to come safely through.

VI

"Fie! Fie! My dear daughter, Mary,
If you are distraught, don't lose your shame.
It's easier for you to get a husband than three brothers.
And praise a hundred-fold to the Virgin Mary that my sons have
come safe."

VII

You would not say that, Mother, indeed if you were with him in
London,
Where I would get a finely fitted cloak imported from Spain,
And suits of clothes surpassing all others, wherever I'd go.

VIII

I've had from him gloves for my hands and rings without number,
And pearls to wear whenever I'd choose to,
Fine shapely boots you've not yet heard me mention,
And hats for my head for outings and sporting events.

IX

I'd have finely milled flour which had been sifted through arches,
Delicious roast beef and games of backgammon,
Spirited stable horses for riding,
And leave to sleep securely between his two arms.

X

Small is the wonder that I am weary with sorrow,
For often I saw you at the door of the courthouse,
Crowds riding by and crowds dismounting,
The tables outspread and the lights never quenched.

XI

Do shiúlíos-sa leat-sa trí bhogra is chruatain,
Agus chuas ar anaithe na farraige móra,
Go Briostó anonn thar n-ais go Lios Tuathail,
Nó go Baile Átha Cliath síos ag foghlaim dhuanta.

XII

Fanaigh uaigh, a chanaithe ghlasa!
Agus ná bídh-se ag siúl ar uaigh mo mharcaigh
Mar is é mo leannán é agus céile mo leaba,
Agus mo chéad-fhear pósta ó bhíos im leanbh.

XIII

A mhná uaisle, nach trua libh mo scéal-sa,
Ag gol go huaigneach ar uaigh mo leannáin.
Go bhfuil craobh dá chuid gruaige agam-sa i gcoimeád.
Agus coileán dá scuainthe fuaighte im cheartlár.

XI

I have walked with you through thick and thin,
Enduring the tempests of the great ocean, over to Bristol and back to
Listowel,[80]
Or over to Dublin to study poetry.

XII

Stay away from him, you green-coloured hawkmoths![81]
Do not be walking on the grave of my hero.
For he is my lover and my bedmate,
And my first wedded husband since I was a child.

XIII

Oh ladies, don't you feel for me pity,
As I weep so sadly on the grave of my loved one.
I have a lock of his hair stowed in safe keeping.
And a puppy from his kennel held fast in my bosom.

---

[80] Listowel — a town in County Kerry.
[81] Hawkmoth — The elephant hawkmoth, "found in dark places and
regarded with aversion. On being discovered, it is instantly killed, as it is
believed to sting cattle severely in the muzzle." (An Irish-English
Dictionary by Rev. Patrick S. Dinneen, MA, Irish Texts Society, 1927)

CAOINE SHEÁIN DE BÚRC

I

Bean Sheáin á chaoine:
A Sheáin de Búrc, mo chúmha trím aeibh thú,
A bhuinneáin úir an chliatháin ghléigil,
Do chúm is gile ná feicim ar aon fhear.
Cé go dtáinís go ró-mhoch ag fógairt an lae chughainn.

II

Tóg do cheann go n-ínnsead scéal duit
Go bhfuilim gan fear, gan mhac, gan aoinne.
Mathshlua mór ag teacht at éileamh.
Beirt ó Lonndain agus triúr ó Éirinn.
Mo thriúr deartháir, agus a ngearáin traochta,
Le páipéir bhreaca go daingean faoi séala,
Ag teacht led phárdún ón Rí saor chughat.

III

Is beag an t-iongnadh dhom-sa bheith go túirseach,
Mar is minic do chonnac-sa ag doras do chúirte,
Mathshlua ag marcaíocht agus mathshlua ag tiúrlacan,
Do bhúird ar leathadh agus do sholuis gan múchadh.

IV

Agus mo mhíle deacair do mharbh, a Bhúrcaigh,
Mo chreach thinn dheacarach nach é Eilic atá it áit-se,
Nó Éamonn ó b'é a b'fhearr díobh.
Nó Toiríolach geal, fionn-dalta mo mháthar,
Agus Seán de Búrc do theacht 'na sláinte.

THE "KEENING" OF JOHN BURKE[82]

I

John's wife lamenting him:
Oh John Burke, my grief for you pierces my heart.
Oh fresh, slender sprout of the lightsome body,
Whiter your waist than I've seen on any man.
Though you have come too soon to announce to us the day.

II

Raise your head until I tell of my plight,
That I am bereft of husband, of child, of everyone.
A great host is coming at your bidding.
Two from London and three from Ireland.
My three brothers, their horses exhausted,
With writs duly sealed,
Bringing from the King a free pardon for you.

III

Little wonder that I am weary with sorrow,
For often I have seen you at the door of the courthouse,
Crowds on horseback and crowds dismounting,
Your tables outspread and your lights unquenched.

IV

Oh a thousand pities your death, my Burke,
My direst regret is that Alec isn't in your place,
Or Éamonn, since he was the best of them.
Or fair-haired Terence, my mother's dear foster-son,
And John Burke to come back alive.

---

[82] Collected from Johanna Kelleher, who told biographer O'Donoghue that
Mary O'Leary composed the whole lament but pretended that the speakers
were John's wife and her mother.

V

Bhí a máthair ag éisteacht léi agus do labhair:
Is baoth an bhean tú, a iníon mh'árann.
Agus má taoi ar buile ná caill do náire.
Is usa fear fháil ná triúr deartháir breátha.
Agus céad moladh le Muire mar is iad mo leinbh-se tháinig.

VI

An bhean arís:
A mháithrín ó, ní déarfá-sa féin sin,
Dá mbeifá-sa aige i nOileáinín Mhaona,
Mar a mbeadh clóca 'á chóriú ins an Spáinn duit,
Plúr mín muilinn dá rilleadh trí áirsibh,
Cead marcaíocht ar eachaíbh stábla,
Agus cead codhladh go cluthair idir a dhá láimh siúd.

VII

"Do raghainn-sea leat ar bogra nó ar cruatain.
Do raghainn-se ar anfa na farraige ruaí leat,
Go Briostó nó go Lios Tuail.
Nó go Baile Átha Cliath na ngeataí móra.
Agus is é mo léan ná deigheas san uaigh leat.
Mh'uchlán! A bhuinneáin, do cheann ar an bhfuarma.

VIII

A mhná uaisle, deinidh slighe dhó, agus tugaidh tosach curtha síos do.
Mar níl aon bhraon ann ach braon dá aoirde.
Fuil tiarnaí agus iarlaí tíre, fuil giústísí go n-umhlaídís daoine.
Agus fuil na nGearalthach 'na lasaraibh tríd sin.

IX

Druidigh uaim, a chanaithe glasa.
Agus ná bídh anuas ar uaigh mo mharcaigh,
Mar is é m'fhear pósta é is mo chéile leaba,
Agus mo chéad leannán ó bhíos im leanbh.
A mhná uaisle, an trua libh mo ghearán,
Ag gol go huaigneach ar uaigh mo leannáin.
Go bhfuil táth dá chuid gruaige agam i gcoiméad.
Agus coileán dá scuaine fuaighte im cheartlár.

V

Her mother was listening to her and spoke:
You are a foolish woman, my daughter most dear.
And if you are distraught, do not lose your shame.
It is easier to find a husband than three splendid brothers.
And a hundred praises to Mary that my sons came safely.

VI

The wife again:
Oh little mother, you yourself would not say that,
If you were with him in London, where a cloak would be prepared in
Spain for you,
Fine milled flour, sifted through arches, freedom to go riding on
stable horses, and to sleep securely between his two arms.

VII

I would walk through thick and thin with you.
I would go with you on the tempestuous sea to Bristol or to Listowel.
Or to Dublin of the large city gates.
And woe is me that I haven't gone into the grave with you.
Alas, my darling, your head on the cold ground.

VIII

Oh ladies, make room for him, and let him begin his rest.
For there is not one drop of blood in him but the noblest.
The blood of lords and earls of the land,
The blood of the judiciary to whom all would curtsy.
And the blood of the Geraldines to blazon through it all.

IX

Get away from me you green-coloured hawkmoths.
And do not settle on the grave of my hero,
For he is my husband and my bedmate,
And the first lover since I was a child.
Oh ladies, do not pity my grieving,
As I weep so lonely on my lover's grave.
A lock of whose hair I have in safe keeping.
And a puppy from his kennel held fast in my bosom.

CAOINE AR LIAM Ó RINN

I

Tá mná tí ag screadaigh i ngleanntaibh Uíbh Laoghaire,
Agus smúit go talamh ar mo Bharra bhreá naofa.
I ndiaidh an mharcaigh seo do cailleadh go déannach,
Is é Liam Ó Rinn, mo mhíle léan é.

II

'S is dúch liom t'athair 's do bhanaltra it éaghmais,
Do chéile leaba 's do leanbh ag glaoch ort.
Cúis faoi ndeara dhom ná raghainn it fhéachaint:
Mar bhínn gach maidean ag faire dom laonnaibh.

III

Crosaim Dia ort a shíneann caolfhear.
Is nár chuirtear sa chill I gcumaoin le chéile,
Ach scailp cois claí gan díon ón spéir ort.
Ná fiú an chúnlaigh mar chlúdach chléibh ort.

LAMENT FOR WILLIAM RING[83]

I

Women are wailing in the glens of Iveleary,
And beloved Gougane Barra[84] is all covered with clouds.
All because of this hero lately departed,
For William Ring, my thousand-fold grief.

II

I feel for your father and mother without you,
For your bedmate and child crying out for you.
The reason why I had not come to see you:
I was every morning on the watch for my dear ones.[85]

III

God be your judge, you who strike down a young man.
And not have him buried along with his comrades in the graveyard,
But in a cleft by a ditch, unscreened from the elements.
With not even moss to cover your breast.

---

[83] Collected from Nora Cronin of Inchibeg, County Cork. The song seems to be incomplete. William Ring was one of the Rockites hanged after the Battle of Keimaneigh.

[84] Gougane Barra — St. Finbarr's mountain hollow, located about 1.6 km to the north of Keimaneigh. The area was placed under the protection of St. Finbarr around 1700 when pilgrimages were made to the sacred isle. St. Finbarr, who died circa 548, was a monk who lived in this locale for a while before making his way south to the River Lee, where he built a monastery. He is the patron saint of Cork. Barry is a latter-day derivation of his name.

[85] Dear ones — a reference to members of Mary O'Leary's family who participated in the Battle of Keimaneigh and were fugitives for some time afterwards.

AN CRÚISCÍN LÁN

I

Maidean áluinn ghréine is mé ar thaobh Cnoc na Buailem,
Do dhearcas cúileann mhaorga, is a bréid fliuch ón luachair.
Bhí gile is finne i n-aonfheacht go gléineach 'na gruanaibh.
Agus d'fhúig sí m'inntin léanmhar, 's is baolach nach buan bhead.
Agus ghabham arís an crúiscin, is bíodh sé lán.

II

D'fhiosras, go béasach den spéirbhruinneal stuama:
"Cá bhfuilid do ghaolta, nó cá taobh as gur ghluaisis?
An bean le fán an tsaol thú gan chéile ar do thuairisc ar fuaimint?
Nó an fior gur tusa Céarnait chuir na treeanmhuilthe ar fuamint?"
Agus ghabham arís an crúiscin, is bíodh sé lán.

III

"A óigfhir mhúinte bhéasach ní haoinne mé dhá nduabhrais,
Ach bean do mhaithibh Gael mé tá léanaithe I gcruatan.
M'ainm cheart 'sí Éire, is Mac Shéarlais am ruaigairt.
Mo bhailtí puirt ag béaraibh an éirli 's an fhuadaigh."
Agus ghabham arís an crúiscin, is bíodh sé lán."

IV

Thugas crotha láimhe dhí is céad fáilte roim mo stuaire.
Cuire stad go lá de go sásta chun suaimhnis.
Go ndéanfainn tinte cnámh di le háthas I mbuaic chnuic.
D'fhonn go mbeadh an lá againn agus cead ráis ar na huaislibh.
Agus ghabham arís an crúiscin, is bíodh sé lán.

THE FULL JUG

I

On a lovely sunny morning by the side of Knocknabooly,
I saw a stately maiden, her robe wet from the rushes.
Pureness and brightness on her cheeks glowed together.
She left my mind in torment, and I fear I shall not endure long.
And let's pass around the jug again, and let it be full.

II

Politely, I asked of the poised lovely lady:
"Who are your relatives, and where do you hail from?
Are you a wandering woman with no husband there to trace you?
Or is it true that you are Cearnet[86] who built solidly the great mills?"
And let's pass around the jug again, and let it be full.

III

"My gentle-mannered young man, I am none of those you have
mentioned,
But a woman of the noble Gaels who is sorely afflicted.
My true name is Erin, by Charlie's son rejected.
My lands possessed by brutes given to plunder and destruction."
And let's pass around the jug again, and let it be full.

IV

I gave her a handshake and a welcome to my fair one.
Asked her to stay till daylight in peace and contentment.
And I'd make for her a bonfire happily on the hilltop.
So we could have our day and the devil take the gentry.
And let's pass around the jug again, and let it be full.

---

[86] Cearnet — the beautiful daughter of a Pictish king of Scotland. She was
loved by King Cormac MacArt of Ireland. Cormac's wife, Ethni Ollamda,
compelled the girl to grind nine pecks of grain every day on a hand-mill.
Bearing Cormac's child, and unable to work at milling, she appealed to the
King who immediately sent to Scotland for men to construct a mill, thus
relieving her from drudgery.

V

"Níl caoi dhom stad go lá agat, cé gur gádh dhom an suaimhneas.
Do chaitheas triall go Clár Luirc mar thánaig le tuairisc,
Go bhfuil Sasanaigh is a n-áltha as an áit seo le ruaigairt.
Agus Clanna Gael 'na n-áitreabh 's is áthas liom rómhair é."
Agus ghabham arís an crúiscin, is bíodh sé lán.

V

"I cannot stay the night with you, though I've need of relaxation.
I must travel to Lorc's Plain[87] for I've come with information,
That the Saxons and their brood here are doomed to extirpation.
And the Gaels to take their mansions, which brings me to exultation."
And let's pass around the jug again, and let it be full.

---

[87] Clár Luirc — Lorc's Plain — poetic name for Ireland. Leary Lorc, son of Iugane the Great, high king of Ireland about 300 AD.

A MHÁIRE NÍ LAOGHAIRE

I

A Mháire ní Laoghaire ó bhéal an Chéama,
Mar a mbíonn os maol dá dhúiseacht,
An amhla éagais, ná hairím éinphioc
De ghuth do bhéil 'á mhúscailt?
Nó an bhfeacaís aoinne ag gabháil, moch nó déannach,
'Sa ghleann so taobh le Diúbhchoill do 'neosad scéal duit ar ghníorta
an tsaol seo
Go raibh Clanna Gael gcúngaireacht?

II

Do chualag scéal duit anois go déannach
O fhideog sléibhe bhí i nDiúchoill,
Go suífa téarma gan moill i nÉirinn
Do chuirfa béir ar geúlaibh;
Go mbeadh Repealers is a bhfórsaí tréana,
Agus cúnamh Dé 'á stiúradh,
Agus buíon an Bhéarla gan fíon gan féasta
Agus stealladh piléar dhá ndúiseacht.

III

Go n-éirí an saol leis an bhfideoig sléibhe 'amuigh
A thug an scéal san chughat-sa
Le grá is le méinn duit thar mná na hÉireann.
A bhláth is a chraobh na n-údar;
Ó bhís chomh héasca agus lách le béaraibh
Is a bhfágaint tréith le púdar,
Tá an cáirde taobh leo le grásta an Aonmhic
Do gheárr an téarma ar dtúis dóibh.

Oh Mary O'Leary[88]

I

Oh, Máire ní Laoire from the mouth of the Céim,
Where the harmless deer are stirring,
Have you really died, for I have not heard one sound from your lips
emerging?
Or have you seen any wayfarer, early or late, in this valley beside
Doughill[89] who would bring any news of life's happenings
That the Gaels were in sore affliction?

II

I have heard some news for you now of late from the golden plover
in Doughill,
That a time would be set at once in Erin when the bears would all be
routed,
That the Repealers[90] would arrive in full array,
And with God's aid to steer them, leave English speakers wineless
and feastless
With a volley of bullets to wake them.

III

Success and long life to that golden plover who brought to you this
story.
In love and friendship, above all, Irish women, oh flower and pride
of authors,
Since you have been so easy and kind to the bears as to lay them low
with powder,
Their day has come by grace of God's son, who first marked their
time of accounting.

---

[88] Collected by Donal Lucey. On the manuscript, now in the Special
Collections department of University College Cork, are the lines: "Mary
Burke of Keimaneigh composed seven stanzas of this song, and Denis
Lynch, Ballyvourney, composed the first and last stanzas."
[89] Doughill — the hill of Doughill, south of Keimaneigh, 474 metres high.
[90] Repealers — followers of Daniel O'Connell in his effort to repeal the Act
of Union.

IV

Beidh stealladh piléar agus pící géara
Dhá gcur 'na méadail bhrúidigh,
Beidh cloch is craobh ortha ó láimh gach aoinne
Agus mallacht Dé ar a gcomplacht,
Beidh siad faoinlag faoi spalladh gréine
Gan neach sa tsaol 'na gcúram
A gcoin 'sa mbéagles is a gcapaill traochta
Gan dúil I ngéim ná i liú acu.

V

Tá dream an áil go céasta cráite
Agus cíos is cáin á dtúrna
Agus búir go táchtmhar ar hallaí bána
Agus deire a gcáirde tabhartha;
Ní bheidh féasta ar chlár dóibh ach prátaí bána
Agus salann lán de bhrúscar,
Is ní bheinn féin seasta le méid a ngátair
Go bhaidís bás gan bhlúire.

VI

Dá mbeinn ar chlár ghlan faoi thobac geárrtha
Is faoi sholus bhán gan múca
Go n-airíonn rás ar an ndream so chráidh sinn
Go n-éiríonn láidir chúcha.
Tá mo shúil lem Máistir ná raghad 'on bhán ghlas
Go bhfeicead tláth an complacht,
Is go mbead 'á n-áireamh i bpollaibh báidhte
Is le faillibh árda 'á rúsca.

IV

A hail of bullets and sharp pike thrusts will pierce their brutish bodies
Sticks and stones from all hand flung and God's curse down upon them.
Faint they will lie under the scorching sun, without a soul in the world to tend them.
Their hounds and beagles and horses spent with no voice or cry left in them.

V

Our people are crushed in dire distress, by rent and taxes broken,
While the boors strut tall in lighted halls, though their respite now is over.
Their "feast" at table will be bare potatoes with salt that's full of rubbish.
Nor content I'll be with all their need until they die of hunger.

VI

If I were being waked, the tobacco cut[91] and candle burning brightly,
And heard our tormentors were on the run, I would rise in strength to smite them.
I pray the Lord I shan't go to the grave till I see that gang prostrated,
And their corpses count in bog holes drowned, or by high hedges laid fast.

---

[91] Cut tobacco — It was the custom in Iveleary, as in other parts of Ireland, to lay the body of a deceased person on boards, or on a bed in the kitchen, with cut-up tobacco on one plate, snuff on another, and a lit candle on the table. The tobacco and snuff were for those attending the funeral, on the understanding they would pray for the deceased.

VII

A mhic an deáthar, do chualag trácht ort
Gur mhaith do cháil id dhúthaigh,
Guidhim séan is áthas is sliocht faoi bhláth ort
A chuirfidh cráiste is fonn ort;
Dá gcastaoi lá orm thú I dti'n tábhairne
Do thabharfainn cárt faoi chúr duit Is crotha láimhe ag ól do sláinte
Agus punch ar chlár go flúirseach.

VIII

'S a mhic an deáthar, nár thuill tú cháineadh
Do bhí fial fáilte flúirseach,
Ní dhéanfa trácht ar a thuille dánta
Táim críona támhach lag brúite;
Bronnaim láithre an chraobh id láimh duit, a bun, a barr, 's a húla,
Is ná caill do chráiste - sa bhliain seo láimh linn
A bheidh uchlán ar bhúraibh.

IX

Go deimhin, a stóraí, má's fíor do ghlórtha, gur dheinis óg arís mé,
Chun tally-ho bheith ar mhná na rógairí d'itheann feoil Dia hAoine;
Is é deir lucht eolais go mbeid siúd brónach, mar gheall ar phóit an tsaol seo.
Ná leanann comhairle na cléire córach, is gabháil an bóthar díreach.

VII

"Oh fine man's son, I have heard of you that at home you are highly
thought of.
May you flourish in joy with heirs at your call, so you'll never flinch
or falter.
If we were to meet at a tavern seat, I'd stand you a foaming quart,
son,
And shake your hand and drink your health, with plenty of punch to
call for.

VIII

"Oh fine man's son who deserved no blame,
You've been princely, frank and noble.
I will no more in verses speak, I'm old, dull, worn, and weak.
I give you at once the victor's branch, its base and tip and laurels.
Keep up your heart, this coming year, the boors will start their
bawling.

IX

"Indeed, my love, if true your words, my youth again you'll find me
To notch the score on the wives of rogues who eat flesh meat on
Fridays.
They say, those who know, those will come to woe who are given to
inebriety,
Who do not heed the upright priests and walk the road that's
righteous."

TÁ GAEIL BHOCHT CRÁIDTHE

I

Tá Gaeil bhocht cráite go céasta cásmhar
Agus cúirt gach lá ortha mar dhúbailt brón,
Clanna sáirfhear dá gcrocha anáirde
'S dá gcur síos láithreach 'sa Croppy-hole;
Tá na loingeas lean díobh dá gcur thar sáile,
Mo chúmha go grá sibh faoi iomad yoke,
Nára fada an cáirde go bhfuighe sibh sásamh -
Is agat-sa atá san, a Rí na gComhacht.

II

Is é chuala ó fháidhí go ndúirt Naomh Seán linn
Go raibh deire an cháirde caite leo,
'S go dtiocfa slaughter ar gach piara másach
Nár ghéill don Pháis is do chaith an phóit;
Aon chaonaí fánach ná tabharfar bás do.
Ag iomchar mála agus é 'na dhóid
'S gan déirc sa láimh sin a thabharfa náid dó.
Ach buala is cáineadh dá mbrú go deo.

III

Is an bhliain seo atá againn 'sea bheidh rírá againn
Taréis búir do thnátha is do charta i ngleo
Beidh tinte cnámha againn ar na mullaíbh árda
Agus adharc le háthas ag seinm ceoil;
Mná agus páistí go mbeid dá dtnátha
Is le clocha an bháin 'sea do leagfaid póirc,
Is le leomhnú an Ártmhic go dtuitfid lánlag
Chomh tiugh le báistigh ar chnoc lá ceoidh.

THE POOR GAELS ARE IN TORMENT[92]

I

The poor Gaels are in torment, afflicted most sorely,
Hauled daily to court to double their woe.
Splendid young men, hanged high on the gallows,
And cast at once into Croppy Hole.[93]
Ships are filled with those being transported.
My grief for you ever, under many a yoke.
Let the respite be short till you get retribution,
And that is in Your hands, Oh Lord of Hosts.

II

I have heard from the prophets what Saint John has told us,
That the time of withholding has drawn to a close.
That ripe for the slaughter are those big-bellied butchers
Who have rejected Christ's Passion for orgies and sport.
Any one of their party surviving the slaughter,
A beggarman's sack in his hand will he hold.
Empty that hand, no alms will it carry,
But beatings and brandings his lot ever more.

III

In this very year, the hubbub we'll witness
When the bears will crumble, crippled by blows.
We'll have bonfires ablaze high on the hilltops
With horns playing music for joy uncontrolled.
Women and children, till they are wearied,
Rocks from the fields at the brutes they will throw.
And if the High Son allows, may these fall in prostration
As thickly as rain on the misty knoll.

---

[92] Collected by Jeremiah A. Cotter. Mary O'Leary is said to have composed this song on her deathbed. One night when she was very ill and her son was sitting by the fire, strangers knocked on the door and asked the son for a drink of water. They sat by the fire for a while, and then began to speak in derogatory terms about the Irish. Mary O'Leary heard them from her bed, called out to her son, and asked him to bring her down to the fireside. He did so, and when she was settled by the fire, she responded to the strangers with this song.

[93] Croppy Hole — the name given to a pit outside the gates of the Cork County Jail where the bodies of hanged prisoners were dumped after execution.

IV

Leaga is leona agus scéile dóite
Go dtí ar an gcóip sin 's a stór 'na measc,
An chroch san córda dá gcur faoi n-a scórnaigh
Agus Dia nár fhórí go mór a gceas
Ceangal comhraic ortha at Oscar cró
Is é bheith ag gabháil go deo ortha go leona' an gad,
Is I n-áirt na n-óigfhear tá sínte ró-lag
An bhuíon go brónach go deo na ngealt.

V

Tá mo shúil lem Mháistir gur gearr an cáirde
Go bhfeiceam lá ortha agus tamall spóirt,
Is go mbeid dá dtnátha gan chúirt gan stáitse
Gan fallaí bána gan fíon gan beoir;
Go mbeidh na mílte lánphoc i n-aon pholl amháin acu
Ar a dtárr anáirde gan chloch gan fód
Agus Gaeil ar chlár glan ag ól mo shláinte
Is mé féinig láithre dá chnaga leo.

VI

Is nár théid 'sa bhán ghlas ná ag tabhairt an fhásaí
Go bhfeicead rás ar lucht bolg mór
Go mbeidh rith i rás ar an ndream seo chrá sinn
Is d'fhúig faoi'n mbráca gach a dtáinig róinn
Nuair a ghabham an lá ortha níl gnó agaibh trácht liom
Ar phiúnt ná ar chárt do chur ar scór
Ach baraillí lána agus iad ar stáitse
Dá dtabhairt to tháinte mar dhí le n-ól.

IV

May scourge and wounding and terror consuming
befall that group in the midst of their store.
The hangman with rope wrapped around their throats,
and the Lord withholding his eyes from their plight.
And in place of our youth left there to languish
May that group be in anguish till Doomsday comes.

V

I pray to my master to shorten the waiting
Till the tables are turned and we can have sport,
When they're wineless and beerless, weakened and wasted,
Left without status and friends in court.
When that swarm of knaves is cast into a quarry,
And their backsides uncovered by sod or stone,
While the Gaels around the table proudly regale me,
And I with them gladly respond to their toast.

VI

May I not be put under, or the green sod put above me
Till I witness the rout of the big-bellied boors,
Till I see running headlong our heartless oppressors,
Who kept in affliction our fathers before.
When that day comes on them, let none of you squabble
About a pint or a quart to be put on the score.
Full barrels brought in and piled on the platforms
Will supply all callers with gallons galore.

'SÉ MO BHRÓINCHRE

Tadhg Bhuí, deartháir Mháire Bhuí, is é an t-amhránaí.

I

'Sé mo bhróinchre nach Dónal is ainm dom fhéin,
Do rórfainn don eorna is do bhainfinn an féar,
Do seolfainn do bhólacht faoi dhuillúir na gcraobh,
Is do thógfainn an ceo so de chogar mo chléibh.

II

Nuair a shuíom os cionn dí is gan pingin im láimh
Buailim síos is aníos is mo hata ar an gclár
Deor an ríorca aoibhinn de sna maithibh is fearr
"Tair aníos, a Thadhg Bhuí, is seo gloine dhuit lán."

III

Má's Tadhg Buí mé tá croí agam is gile 'ná an chailc,
Is lem mhínchro do scríonn-se litir i gceart
Tá dís de mhná caoinleacht ag iomaí liom seal
Is, fóríor níneach! Is díobh-san an tubaist 's an tart.

IV

Tart gránda atá im dhea-se agus imirim beart
Ar chúig cárta nó ar tháiplis chó cliste le fear
Bhéarfinn árthach ón Spáinn liom cois imealla seal
Is croí cráite ag mnaoi an táirne ná tugann dara searc.

V

Searc seanbhan na mallrosc dob fhada mín géar
Gan amhras thar abha tuile b'fhada í mo léim;
Leabhaireacht mo leabhairchnís ag fear amhail laoch,
Agus labhairt na seacht dteangach is blasta do léim.

VI

Do léinn stair Bhéarla nó Laidin go binn
'Sé mo léirchre ná féadaim bheith i n-aice na dí;
Mo léine dem thaobh ag mnaoi an leanna mar dhíol,
'S nuair a ghlaom tuille 'sé deir, 'seáin atharra gill.

IT'S MY DEEP REGRET

Tadhg Bhuí, brother of Mary O'Leary, is the singer

I

It's my deep regret that I am not Donal by name
I would clear ground for barley and I'd mow the hay.
Your cattle I'd lead beneath leafy trees,
And shake off this cloud that mars my heart's ease.

II

When I sit by the bar, not a coin in my hand,
I stamp up and down, my hat on the stand.
Says the right regal hero, the best of his class:
"Come on up, Tadhg Buí, for you a full glass."

III

If I am Tadhg Buí, my heart is quite white,
And with my fine hand, a fair letter I'd write.
Two smooth-cheeked maids are vying to be first.
My heart's grief, they're the reason of my downfall and thirst.

IV

A vile thirst pursues me and with cards I play tricks
With the five or backgammon, as keen as the next.
Vessels from Spain I would bring to the cove,
And heart's torment on the barmaid who refuses me a drink.

V

Long and keenly I've courted the slow-gazing maids.
Long indeed, my leap over the river in spate,
My litheness of limb a hero would make.
And the speech of seven languages I would fluently read.

VI

English or Latin, quite well I could read.
It pains me to be unable to reach for a beer.
The shirt of my back's with the barmaid in pawn.
And when I call for a drink, she says: "Pledge me some more."

VII

Tá mo cheallta sa gclampar 's is minic sin bhí
Ag lucht leannta 'gus brannda 'gus beathuisce dhíol
Nuair a spalltar mé pleangcaim an canna faoi thrí
Is ní bhfaghainn beann ar mo labhartha ná blaiseadh na dí.

VIII

Blaisim deoch i gCaiseal is i bPortláirge thíos
Is d'fhág san gan airgead ná ór mé, fóríor!
Níl bean leanna ó Chaiseal go Béal Átha na Líog
Ná fuil m'ainm-se, cé taircaisne le rá, Tadhg Buí.

IX

Má's Tadhg Buí mé bíodh 'fhios agaibh-se mar tá -
Go ndíolfainn an bríste dá bhfeicinn an gá,
Ag bríde na rínrosc ba mhinic mé ar lár,
Is I gCill Muire dhíogas an baraille lán.

VII

My pledges are impounded as often they've been
By sellers of whiskey and brandy and beer.
When parched, I bang three times on my cane.
But nobody heeds me or offers a dram.

VIII

I drink in Cashel and in Waterford,
Which has left me, alas, without silver or gold.
No barmaid from Cashel to Bealanaleague
But scornfully utters my name, Tadhg Bhuí.

IX

If I am Tadhg Bhuí, then know how things stand,
I would sell of my breeches, if the need would demand.
I've been often left flat by yon pensive-eyed maid,
And down in Kilmurry, a whole barrel I've drained.

A Dhiarmuid Uí Laoghaire

I

A Dhiarmuid Uí Laoghaire, dúirt ainnir na gcraobh liom
Go dtaineadh do scéimh léi is do tslí
Ach gurab é deir a gaolta d'á dtugaidís spré dhuit
Ná cuirfá-sa í i n-éifeacht ná i gcrích
Mar go bhfuileann tú éadtrom aerach id tslí
Tugtha do bhéithibh is do bhraonachaibh dí
Is gurab é deir gach aoinne go rabhais ar an réice
Ba mhó bhí I nUíbh Laoghaire led linn.

II

Admhuím féinig go bhfuilim buille aerach
Is gur dhúthchas dom é ón gCloinn mBuí
Is ná creid-se ód ghaolta dá dtugaidís spré dhom
Ná cuire í i néife is i gcrích;
Do chrafainn, do réabhfainn, do dhéanfa an claí
Is do bhainfinn an féar gan mo ghéaga a shnoí
Do chóraceóinn aon fhear ar lár pháirc an aonaigh
Is ní féarr mar a bhrágfainn cailín.

III

Go deimhin féin a shéimfhir, do shiúlóinn an saol leat
Ach go ndéarfaoi gur bhaoth é mo ghnó,
Gur mó ainnir chiúin bhéasach gur gheallais ód bhéal di
A malairt ná déanfá go deo,
Is dá gcastaoi ar a chéile sinn féin I dti'n óil
Is go n-áireóinn mo spré dhuit is nár mhéinn leat mo shórt
Bhea mo dhaidín ag éad liom is mo mháithrín ag pléi liom,
Is go bhfága mé ag géarghol go deo.

118

OH JEREMIAH O'LEARY

Jeremiah was the oldest brother of Mary O'Leary

I

Oh Jeremiah O'Leary, to the ringleted maiden,
Your looks and your ways do excel,
But her people doubt that, given the dowry, you would spend it
wisely and well.
For you are lighthearted, free of all care
Fond of the damsels and sipping of ale.
That of rakes, it is stated, you are the greatest
Of all in Iveleary in your day

II

Freely, I state it, I am somewhat carefree,
For that is the nature of folks of Clan Bhuí.
But let not your folks doubt it, if given the dowry
That I wouldn't spend it wisely.
Indeed, I'd mow the meadow and not chop off my limbs.
I'd fight any man at the fair on the green,
And as freely I'd court a colleen.

III

Indeed, my kind man, I would walk through life with you,
Were it not to be judged a foolish deal for me.
There is many a quiet, mannerly maiden.
You promised explicitly you would never deviate from your word.
Perhaps if we met in the alehouse alone.
And I handed you the dowry and me you'd disown.
My dad would be raging, my mother upbraiding.
And you'd leave me in tears ever more.

IV

Go deimhin féin, a spéirbhean, dá siúlófá an saol liom
Ní déarfá gur bhaoth é do ghnó
I dtaobh seafaidí sléibhe 'amuigh 'á n-áireamh dom fhéinig
Cé gur mór iad ag céad fear dom shórt;
B'fhearra liom spéirbhruinneal bhéasach dheas óg
Go dtaine a scéimh liom, a méinn is a gnó
'Na sparán le ladharnach nó é fháil dom ó bhaothrach
Nár ól riamh aon raol I dti'n óil.

V

Féach-se ar mo mhuinntir, mo cháirde, is mo shínsear
Nár ghéill riamh do stríoca I dti'n óil
Ach ag imeacht go fíochmhar faoi theasmhach na bruíne
Bíonn maide agus claíomh ghlía 'na ndóid,
'Na dhéidh siúd bíonn saill agus fíonta acu ar bórd
Agus clanna na dtíosach ag suí síos 'na gcomhair,
Ná creid-sa ód mhuinntir dá mbeidís 'á innsint
Ná gur mar sin a chífar sinn fós.

IV

Indeed, my fair one, if you'd share my way then,
You'd never feel foolish, or fear to hand over cattle — to me a slight
matter.
Though many would value the deal,
I'd rather a gracious young mild-mannered maid,
With beauty to please me and skill at her trade,
Than a purse-proud Virago or miserly matron,
Who never drank sixpence worth of ale.

V

Look at my clansmen, my friends and companions
Who in the tavern to no one would yield.
They would rush to attack in the heat of the battle,
With cudgel in hand or wielding a sword.
Yet with wines and meats their board is replete.
And children well cared for sit down to eat.
So don't heed your parents if they should complain,
Our life still will bear fruit sweet."

COIS ABHANN GHLEANNA AN GHAORTHAIDH

Diarmuid Mac Séamais Uí Chrochúir is é an t-amhránaí. Deirtear gur freagradh an t-amhrán seo ar an amhrán a cheap Máire Bhuí gurab ainm do "Tá Gaeil Bhocht Cráidthe."

I
Cois abhann Ghleanna an Ghaorthaidh is Claedeach na gCígheanna
Is mé ag déanamn mo smaointe go fíormhoch 'sa ló,
Le taithneamh geal na gréine
Ó Phoebus im thimcheall
Ar gnéagaibh gach crainn duille
Is binnghuth ne n-éan;
An uair so ar fad do scaip mo chicah
Le fuaim gach sean ba cheart i gcian
Le suairceas aitis ag teacht le mian
Agus le saorchantainn cheoil
Trím chúrsa go ráinig liom
Báinchnis i bpearsain ghrínn
I lonnramh sa i mbreághthacht
'Sí an stáidbhruinneal mhódhmail

II
Dob fhada dlaoitheach dréimreach a craobh chasta chíortha
A ciabhfholt na ndlaoithe léi ag síneadh go feór
Na mbeartaibh righthe néamhrach
Go péarlach go soillseach
Go slaodhmar go frínseach
Na mínaltaibh óir
Go dualach cochlach feachtha fighe
Go buacach barrfhionn daithte ag tíocht
Go scuabach cruthach slamar ghrianmhar
Mar ré ghlain gan cheo
Go búclach tiugh fáinneach
'Na táithibh léi mar amhail *fleece*
Ba chlúmhail le háthas thug Jason ar bórd

BY THE RIVER OF GLENAGEARY

A response by Jeremiah MacJames O'Connor to Mary O'Leary's song, "The Poor Gaels Are in Torment."

I

By the river of Glenageary and the Paps of Clydagh[94]
As I was meditating, quite early in the day
The bright rays from Phoebus[95] enveloped me completely
And from the branching treetops came the birds' sweet lay
Then did gloom vacate my soul, as echoed true each sound of old
With joy on joy as with could hold while matchless music played
As on I strolled there did appear a form fair in outline clear
In brightness and in splendour, she is the gentle, stately maid

II

Long, ringleted, wavy, her tresses combed so carefully
The plaited strands were reaching down to the floor
In banded tufts intriguing, with pearly tints a-gleaming
Tumbling to the fringes in fine folds of gold
Curling, flounced, of flexing weave, in buoyant sun-tipped tripping leaps
In sweeping, shapely, shimmering heaps, like the clear moon's glow
So luxurious her ringlets like the Fleece, close-fitting
Which gleefully the victor Jason[96] took on board

---

[94] Paps of Clydagh — two peaks in the Derrynasaggart Mountains, close to the Cork-Kerry border.
[95] Phoebus — literally, "the radiant one." In Greek mythology, an epithet of Apollo used in contexts where the god was identified with the sun or as a descendant of the Titaness Phoebe, his grandmother. The Romans venerated him as Phoebus Apollo.
[96] Jason — in Greek mythology, the son of the king of Iolcos in Thessaly, and leader of the Argonauts in the quest for the Golden Fleece.

III

Ar a haighthe leathan aolchruith
Bhí caolmhala shníghte caortha agus lítis
Ag coimheascar 'na cló gach glasra gur chlaochluigh
A claonrosc gan teimheal chins a déid mhion 'na gcírghlain
Ba bhinn blasta a beol anuas a brághaid mar shneachta ar shliabh
A guaille eálga i mbarra tiaghann ba chruaidh a mama geal ar chliabh
Ar a haolchnis gan smól d'fhúig lag na táinte
Le grádh searc dá pearsain ghrinn agus Cúpid gur sháigh sleagh
Trím lár-sa gan dóid

IV

D'fhiosras den réiltean: 'An tú Venus 'na maoidhtear
Nó péarla an chroidhe ghlas
Ó Aeneas gan ghó?
an tú Lasair ghlan nó Hélen
Thug léirsgrios na Traoi thoir
Do shaothruigh Mac Prím leis
Thar tuinnmhuir ar bórd?
an tú an Uathmhar chrothach ba chasta ciabh
Nó an tsuaircbhean chailce a leag an Fhiann
Le fuath don fhear a lean 'na diaidh
Is é tréan-Tailc Mhac Treóin?
An tú Juno nó an Phlánaid
Nó an bháb a thug gean do Naois
Le nár túrnadh na táinte
Nó Ceárnait i gcló?"

V

D'fhreagair blasta an réiltean: "Níor léir dhuit gur sídhe me
Is gaol damh-sa Impire 'gus righthe na slógh
Mh'ainm cheart 'si Éire is mo chéile gur díbreadh
Gan téada gan chaoirse le dí-mheas ón gcoróinn
Beidh uaisle is fiatha ag teacht a gcian
Go cuanta mara ar bharca ag triall buailfid catha i mbailtibh thiar
'S is tréan a leagfaid póirt
Beidh brúidigh gan fhaghálthas
I n-áitreabh úd Chlanna Gaoidheal
I gcúigíbh Inis Fáilbhe is is áthas mo sceol"

III

Oh forehead fair, were pencilled eyebrows fine and slender
The berries' red with lily on her features strove
All nature's green grew dimmer before that peerless vision
Her teeth in dainty splendour and sweet lips like the rose
Her neck like snow on mountain crests,
Firm and full her fair white breasts, as on a flawless mould
Myriad hearts lie wounded for love of her clear beauty
And an arrow forth Cupid has pierced through my own

IV

I asked the fair maiden, "Are you Venus, the famous
Or Pearl of the Great Heart from Aeneas of Old?
Or Lasair pure, or Helen the cause of Trojan quelling
Whom Paris from her dwelling brought with him on board?
Are you the dread ringleted one, or the maid who left Fionn's men
undone
For hate of him who tracked her home, the brave Talc MacTreoin
Are you Juno or Blathnaid,[97] or the girl who loved Naoise
Through whom the hosts have fallen, or Cearnet once more?"

V

Fluently spoke the fair one:
"You saw not I am of Geary, to the Emperor related, and kings of the
hosts
My rightful name is Eire and exiled my mate is, friendless and
forsaken
Scorned and dethroned
But afar the chiefs will rally round, for sheltered bays their barks are
bound
And fast will fall the forts
The brutes will be deprived of the homelands of Ireland's sons
With Innisfail rejoicing as the joyous news unfolds

---

[97] Blathnaid — in Celtic legend, she was the reluctant wife of Curai Mac
Daire. She loved Cuchulainn , her husband's rival. She revealed the secret
entrance to her husband's fortress to him by milking her cow and letting the
milk run down the hill into a stream. Cuchulainn followed the stream, raided
the fortress and rescued Blathnaid.

VI

Beidh Barters, Waggit, Davis
Beamish agus Beecher
Egar agus Gielding
Ag síor-shileadh dheor
Beidh Herbert, Wallis, Leader
Réinigh and Rídigh
Déinigh agus Faoitigh
Cínsigh agus Stowel
Beidh Townsend, Hassett, Orpen, Speers
Gorden, Atkins, Lantoneers,
Gúlaigh, Grainger, Johnson, Seers,
Aires, Bland is Bowen
Crookigh agus Lawtons
Travers, Kilcoffer, Fielding
Hungford agus Hawksaigh
Baldwin agus Dóid

VII

Is i mBanba beidh léirscrios
'Dir thréadta Chailbhin chaoithigh
Mar a dhéanadar na hIosraels
Is Maois aca beo
Nuair a chartuigh insa tréanmhuir
Na hÉigipts gan bhrigh ionnta
La haontoil Mhic Íosa
Do shín slat 'na dhóid
Beidh Bóna ag teacht chun catha rian
Na sluaighte dragan ag teacht 'na dhiaidh
Ag tuargain ghalla nár sheachain riail
Ach craos agus póit
Beigh Úird Mhuire ag rádh a gceacht
Is dáin bhinne cantainn ghrinn
Agus Priúnsa dhon Árdfhuil
Go bhfágfaid a gcoróinn

VI

"From Barters, Waggit, Davis, Beamish, and Beecher Egar, also
Gielding
Constant tears will flow
So Herbert, Wallace, Leader, Reaneys and the Readys
The Whites and the Deaneys, Kenzies too and Stowel
So too from Townsend, Hassett, Orpen, Spears
Gordon, Atkins, Latoneers
Gooleys, Grainger, Johnson, Seers
Aires and Bland and Bowen
The Crooks and the Lawtons, Travers, Kilcoffer, Fielding
The Hungfords and the Hawkses, Baldwin and the Doads

VII

"And in Banba will be havoc, 'mid the flock of foreign Calvin
As in Israel it happened, with Moses to the fore
As Egypt's hosts were caught fast, cast helpless in the waters
While the rod of God's anointed in outstretched hands He holds
To the battle front will Bonaparte lead warrior hosts all poised to
start
To crush our foe who cared for naught but gorging and carousing
Mary's monks will chant their praise
In sweet hymns their voices raise
And the Prince of blood royal will receive the crown

APPENDIX A

LAMENT FOR ART O LEARY

Art O'Leary was Munster's most celebrated folk hero of the eighteenth century. Born circa 1747 near Macroom, Co. Cork, he was the son of Conchobhar O'Laoire of Ballymurphy, one of the signatories to the will of Cornelius O'Leary of Carrignacurra. This establishes Art O'Leary's Iveleary connection.[98]

Art went soldiering to Europe in his teens, and returned about 1767 with the rank of captain. His remarkable physique and athletic appearance caught the eye of a young widow from Iveragh in Co. Kerry, Eibhlín Dhubh Ní Chomhnaill (Dark-haired Eileen O'Connell) - aunt of the Catholic rights activist Daniel O'Connell. She saw Art on the streets of Macroom, and fell in love with him, as she describes in her poem *Thug mo chroí taithneamh duit*. The pair got married, against the will of Eibhlín's relatives, and set up house at Raghleagh (Rath Laoich) near Macroom. For about five years Art, with his proud and fearless bearing, was a thorn in the flesh of the local Protestant ascendancy. He became embroiled with a neighbouring Protestant landowner, Abraham Morris of Hanover Hall, the High Sheriff of Cork.

One account suggests the sheriff wanted to confiscate a champion racehorse owned by O'Leary. Under the Penal Laws — the legislation enacted by the Ascendancy-controlled Irish parliament to prohibit Catholics from owning land or property — no Catholic was allowed to own a horse valued at more than £5. However, Art refused to give up his racehorse.

Art was killed in an encounter with Morris's men at Carriganima on May 4, 1773. Two years beforehand, an exchange of notices in the *Cork Evening Post* had indicated the extent of the rift between the two.

On Oct. 7, 1771, Morris inserted the following announcement:

> Whereas Arthur Leary of Raghleagh, a fellow of character, most notoriously infamous, did, in the evening about 9 of the

---

[98] See Appendix B, IV, below.

clock, on Saturday the 13th July last make an attempt on my life at my dwelling, house in Hanover-Hall, and wounded one of my servants, and feloniously took from him a gun my property which he carried off for which crimes and several others the said Leary now stands indicted in the Crown Office of this court. Now, I do promise a reward of £20 to any person who will apprehend the said Leery and lodge him in the county gaol within twelve months from this date.

Twelve days later, Art O'Leary issued his reply:

Whereas an advertisement dated the 7th of October 1771 has appeared in the Cork Evening Post and signed Abraham Morris, offering a reward of £20 to any person who shall apprehend Arthur Leary of Raghleagh (whom Mr. Morris modestly states is 'a fellow of character most notoriously infamous') and lodge him in the county jail within twelve months from the date thereof for an attempt on his life, wounding one of his servants and feloniously taking from the said servant a gun the property of Mr. Morris.

Now the said Arthur Leary in order to set forth the transaction to which Mr. Morris alludes in a fair and true light, and to remove any prejudice which might have been conceived against him by the public, from Mr. Morris's untrue and disingenuous statement thereof; asserts that having occasion to apply to Mr. Morris, as a magistrate relative to some law proceedings, he did for that purpose about 7 o'clock in the evening of July 13th last, repair to Hanover-Hall, the seat of Mr. Morris, and there in a very modest and respectful manner communicate to him the purport of his complaint, and who without the least cause of provocation fell into a furious rage and made use of very indecent, abusive, and ungentlemanlike language to the said Leary, who thereupon quitted his house and was returning home.

Before he got down the avenue he observed Mr. Morris and John Mason his servant each armed with a gun, pursuing him down the avenue, and when Mr. Morris advanced within twenty yards of the said Leary, he presented his gun at, and shot and wounded him in the hand, whereupon the said John Mason advanced close up to said Leary and presented his gun at him, which said Leary most providentially wrested from him before he had time to perpetuate that crime in the commission of which his master not intentionally failed and afterwards committed the same gun into the hands of one of his Majesty's Justices of the Peace, and soon after lodged an information against this Mr. Morris for the violent assault and attack upon his life.

It is therefore humbly requested that the public in general and particularly that respectable body of Gentlemen the Members of the Muskerry Constitutional Society will suspend their judgment until the merits of this case shall be inquired into by a fair and impartial trial by law.

Dated at Raghleagh, October 19, 1771.

ARTHUR LEARY.

The following is a translated excerpt from the last section of Eibhlín Dhubh Ní Chomhnaill's lament for her dead husband:[99]

I loved you steadfastly the day I spied you first,
At the gable-end of the market-house,
My eye observed you well,
My heart warmed to you,
I stole away from my dear one with you,
And went far away with you.
I had no regrets.
You put a parlour whitening for me,
Rooms a-brightening;
An oven reddening,
Brick-loaves a-baking,
Roast meat on spits for me,
Beeves a-slaughtering
Sleep on eiderdown,
Until the milking-hour,
Or later, if I wished.

My own beloved one, my heart remembers now
That fine spring afternoon,
How well it suited you:

---

[99] Extract from *Danta Ban: Poems of Irish Women, Early and Modern*, selected and translated by P.L. Henry (Mercier Press, 1991).

A hat with golden band,
A sword with silver hilt,
A spirited right hand,
The prance of cavalry
Inspiring mortal fear ·
In a treacherous enemy;
You were prepared for ambling
On your slender, white-faced horse.
The English used bow to earth to you,
Not for your own good,
But for very dread,
Though 'twas by them you fell,
My soul, my dearest one!

My own beloved one!
And when they come home to me,
Little Conor the affectionate,
The baby, Fear O Leary,
They will quickly ask
Where I left their father,
I will say, in my misery,
I left him in Killnamartery
They will call upon their father
And he will not be there to answer.

My own beloved one!
I would not believe you died,
Till your horse came up beside me ·
With reins to earth sliding,
Your heart's blood on its side-face ·
And from there to the polished saddle,
Where you would sit or stand upright.

I gave one leap to the threshold,
A second to the gateway
The third leap to the saddle.
I quickly clapped my hands
And made off at high speed,
As well as I was able,
Till at a stunted furze bush
I found you dead before me,

Without pope or bishop,
Without priest or cleric
To read a psalm over you,
Only an old withered crone
That spread the skirt of her cloak on you
Your blood was pouring to the ground,
I did not wait to cleanse it,
But with my hands I drank it up.

My love for evermore!
And rise up as before,
And come with me homewards.
We'll slaughter fattened cattle;
Invite many to the party,
We'll have music playing,
And then I'll dress your bed for you
With sheets all snow-white.
And fine speckled coverings
That will bring out the sweat
In place of the cold you caught.

Eibhlín brought Art's body to Killnamartery because burial was forbidden in monastic ground. Several years later, the body was moved to the family tomb at the abbey in Kilcrea. One of Art's grandsons, Goodwin Richard Purcell O'Leary, became Professor of Materia Medica at Queen's College, Cork, and was a welcome guest at the Courts of Sweden and Denmark because of his offer to bring 100 Irishmen, mounted and accoutered, to the aid of Denmark, then threatened by the might of Austria and Prussia. After he died in Manchester in 1876, Goodwin Richard Purcell O'Leary's remains were brought home to be laid in his grandfather's tomb in Kilcrea.

APPENDIX B[100]

I

IN NOMINE DEI, AMEN[101]

I Fineen McDaniel Leary, of Gortaneadin in the parish of Inchigeelagh, Barony of Muskerry and County of Cork, Yeoman, in my perfect sense and memory, though weak of body, do make my last will and last testament as followeth, the 2nd day of January, 1663:

Imprimis: I commit my soul to the Almighty and do desire my body may be buried in my parish Church of Inchigeelagh. For the love and natural affection I ever bore unto Tadhg O'Leary of Carrignacurra, and for the like love and affection my father had unto Cnogher[102] O'Leary, father unto the said Tadhg, and specially in consideration of a considerable sum of money my father received from Cnogher O'Leary (the said Tadhg's father) upon condition the reversion should be in him and his heirs, of what estate we had, my father and I die without issue male. I leave and bequeath unto the said Tadhg O'Leary all my right by the, and interest in, the five gnives of Gortaneadin, Tooreennanean, and Lower Gortnalour, to inure unto him the said Tadhg, his heirs and assignees for ever.

If the said Tadhg O'Leary does recover the said five gnives[103] from his Magties, or any other therein concerned, I desire the said Tadhg O'Leary, whom I do appoint my executor of this my last will, to pay unto my natural son Cnogher O'Leary the sum of ten pounds in cattle or money, in eavarale gales. To pay unto Cnogher

---

[100] I have modernized the spelling in some parts of these documents to make them more readable.

[101] Latin — "In the Name of God, Amen."

[102] Cnogher — an early anglicized form of Conchobhar or Crochúr (Conor or Cornelius).

[103] Gnive (also gneeve) — a land measure amounting to one-twelfth of a ploughland, i.e. fifty acres. In early English law, a ploughland, also called a "hide," varied in size but commonly consisted of about 120 acres, enough land to sustain a household.

O'Moynihan, two shillings. To Daniel Morgigh O'Leary, two pounds. To Mahon McShane, two shillings. To Síle Ní Daniel O'Leary, half a barrel of oatenmeal. To recover towards the payment of the above sums, twelve shillings and seven pence due to me from Daniel McDonagh Carthy. To recover from John Ryne, four shillings and sixpence.

This is my last will, which I desire to be attested by the now witnesses:

Fineen O'Leary (X — his mark)
Being present:
Owen Field, Daniel McCarthy (X — his mark)

II

WILL OF FINEEN O'LEARY

In the name of God, I, Fineen McTadhg Óg O'Leary, being impotent and weak of body, but sound of wit and memory, do make this my last will and testament in manner following:

Imprimis: I bequeath unto Síle Ní Leary, my married wife, the third part of my lands, in lieu and consideration of her jointure during her natural life, together with all my corn and household stuff, and also all my cattle, great and small.

Ite: I bequeath unto Tadhg O'Leary half a gnive of my said land, after the death of the said Síle, according the lease given by me unto the said Tadhg.

Ite: I further bequeath unto the said Tadhg O'Leary, his heirs, executors and assignees, one gnive and three parts of a gnive of my said land for the term of fifty and one years from my death for being in consideration of many good gnives and moneys and other goods by me received at the hands of the said Tadhg and Margaret Leary, his mother.

Ite: I bequeath unto Fineene McTadhg Leary, my grandchild, half a gnive more of my said land after my said wife's death, together with three arts of a gnive more of the said land after my one death, being in consideration of twelve pounds sterling by me promised unto Ellen Ní Fineen, the said Fineen's mother, my one daughter for the term of forty one years, paying his proportion of the Earl of Clan Carthy chief rent, and all other contrg. Charges payable thereout.

In witness whereof I have hereunto put my hand and seal, the 13th of April 1670.

Fineen O'Leary (X — his mark, seal)
Being present: George Lombard, Dom. Thyre, John Roche.

I do hereby certify to all whom it may concern that I have picked and appointed my well beloved friend Tadhg McAuliffe Leary of Gurteen, in the parish of Inchigeelagh, to procure and get an administration out of ye bishop's court in my name, and in the name of those named along with me in my husband's will, late deceased, by name Fineen McTadhg Óg O'Leary of the above mentioned lands as appears in the will and the ministration.

I do further impound and authorize my said well-beloved friend Tadhg McAuliffe Leary to act, do and proceed for me and in my name in this behalf, and in all my tenements, whatsoever in as large and ample a manner as if I were personally present myself, all which is and will be allowed, confirmed, and ratified by me as witness my hand, the 13th of February, 1672.

Gilyin Shane als Leary (X — her mark)
Being present: Auliffe Og O'Leary, Tadhg Og O'Leary (X — his mark)

III

WILL OF DERMOT O'LEARYE ALS[104] BOY[105], 1700

In the name of God, Amen.

The will and last testament of Dermod Lery Als Boy of Inchideraille and Derrynaglass:

I Dermod Lery Als Boy of Inchideraille and Derrynaglass in the parish of Inchigeelagh and County Cork do hereby, at my last will and testament, will and bequeath my soul to God Almighty, and body to the earth from whence it came.

And as for my worldly effects, I hereby will and bequeath all my worldly substance (viz.) all my goods, chattels, debts, dues and demands, deeds, leases, assignments, profits of lands, rents or tenements, which is now present or in my custody or possession, or shall hereafter come to the advantage or profit (in any way) to my heirs or executors, I do hereby will and bequeath all these and every of these at the will and pleasure and command of Ellen my wife, and do hereby will and bequeath her the said Ellen to be sole heir and executor of all these and every of the forementioned effects (viz.) goods, chattels, lands, leases, debts and demands, deeds, assignments, profits of rents or tenements during her life, to be and belong unto her, and at her disposal, all moneys, claims and interests hereditary belonging to my sons or daughters, alleading thereunto notwithstanding, and that the said Ellen shall pay and make satisfaction for all debts, bills, dues and demands, lawfully (in any way) due from me to any person or persons, and likewise do hereby declare to be due unto me as followeth (viz.):

	£ – s. – d. – g.
From Bryn Dorris	1 – 0 – 0 – 0
From Cornelig McDer. McArthy	
From Daniel McTadhg McDermot	1 – 13 – 0 – 0
From Aulif McDono. and his brother	0 – 6 – 3 – 0

---

[104] Als — an abbreviation of "alias," meaning "in other words."
[105] Boy — an anglicized form of Clan Bhuí.

$$0 - 4 - 0 - 0$$

Dermot O'Leary Als Boy (X — his mark)
Being present: Tadhg Marinane, Donogh Croneene.
Probate of this will was granted the 25th July 1700.

IV

ABSTRACT OF WILL OF CORNL. O'LEARY OF CARRIGNACURRA, GENTLEMAN, 1753

Bequeaths to son Timothy O'Leary all leasehold lands of Carrignacurra, as also household goods and cattle, except £400 to my two daughters, Nelly and Julan, carrying 6% interest. Should they cohabit with my said son, then she or they are to pay him £8 per year for their diet, he allowing them £4 off interest for their clothing.

Bequeaths to daughter Ellen O'Leary one English shilling as a memorial of her bad behavior and disobedience. To niece Mary Leary (alias McAuliffe), two newmilk cows. Leaves £20 to be disposed of for charitable purposes for the good of my soul, as my executors shall think fit. My will is that my two daughters shall have the use of two riding horses as long as they live with my son. Cornelius O'Leary of Ballymurphy,[106] Dennis O'Leary of Cooluggane, Charles O'Leary of Demryancannig, and Timothy O'Leary of Glasheen as executors.

Witnessed by: Donogh O'Leary, Charles Carthy, John O'Leary.

---

[106] Father of Munster folk hero, Art O'Leary.

V

ABSTRACT OF WILL OF ELIZABETH O'LEARY THE ELDER, 1759, OF GLASHEEN.

Bequeaths soul to God. Body to be buried as her children shall think proper. All her worldly substance to her best friend Morgan Donovan of Ronan's Grove, beseeching him to make over the profits between her four children, Henry, Daniel, Richard and Elizabeth, and making last request to him to act as a friend. 14 April, 1759.

Witnesses: Tim Leary, Dennis O'Leary, Morgan Donovan renounced his right. Probate granted to Tim O'Leary in the Parish of Inchigeelagh, as husband of Elizabeth O'Leary, the only daughter.

VI

EXCERPT FROM THE CALENDAR OF THE GRANTS OF LANDS (FIANTS) OF ELIZABETH (1533-1603)

(1) 2264, 1573, 8th May.

Pardon ** to Cnogher M'Dermod O'Leary of Inchigeelagh in consideration of their having given 131 cows for the army in Muster, and in consideration of their having released all debts due to them by the Crown, and all exactions and cesses for the Queen's Service in Munster, which had been taken from them.

(2) 3121 (2623).

Grant under Queen's letter 2 (2), May XIX. 1577 to Cormock McTadhg McCarthy of the whole preceptory of Morne Alias Manister ne Monye, Co. Cork **** rectories **** of Inchigeelagh.

(3) 6467 (5237).

Pardon to Cormac McDermot McCarthy of the Blarnin, Co. Cork, Esq., **** Cormac McTadhg McOwen of Macroom, **** Dermot Roe O'Leary of Inchigeelagh, and Lisagh O'Leary of same, gentlemen — Eilis ni Crowley, wife of O'Leary. Sheila ni Morrough, wife of Dermot Roe O'Leary.

Conditions: Provisions for security to be given before the President, etc. of Munster, and provided that they appear and submit themselves before the President, Chief and Second Justice and Attorney of the Province of Munster within three months, and be sufficiently bound with sureties to keep the peace and answer at sessions in the several counties where they dwell when called to answer the demands of any subject according to justice. The pardon shall not extend to any in prison, or on bail to appear, or any priests, seminarians or Jesuits, nor include intrusion on Crown lands or debts to the Crown. The exception for murder is added to the usual clause excluding from pardon treason against the Queen's life. 17 Feb, XLIII (1600-1).

APPENDIX C

I

CENSUS OF 1821
TOWNLAND OF TURREENANANE

(1) — Jeremiah Leary[107]	70	farmer	25 acres
Joana "	70	wife	
Corns. "	29	son	
Richard "	26	son	
John "	41	son	
Jeremiah "	6	grandson	
May "	10	grandaughter	
Ellen "	7	"	
Eliain "	6	"	
Joana "	4	"	
Timothy Coakley	26	house servant	
Hanna "	26	house maid	
Jeremiah Cronin	70	strolling beggar	
(2) — Jeremiah Leary[108]	35	farmer	12.5 acres
Ellen "	31	wife	
John "	4	son	
Joane "	5	daughter	
Mary "	2	"	

---

[107] Father of Mary O'Leary.
[108] Mary O'Leary's brother.

TOWNLAND OF INCHIMORE

James Burke	50	farmer 150 acres or 3 gns.
Mary "[109]	47	wife
Ml. "	25	son
Rd. "	23	son
James "	27	son
Elick "	17	son
Patk. "	13	son
Ellen "	15	daughter
Mary "	8	"
Joanna "	6	"
Ellen "	22	daughter-in-law
Mary "	1	grand-daughter
Daniel Leary	19	nephew
Timothy Lehane	30	house servant
Julian Leary	22	house maid.

TOWNLAND OF INCHIBEG

John Burke[110]	28	farmer
Honna "	24	wife
Richard "	1.5	son
Honna "	10	first cousin
Daniel Coakley	10	in character of a cowboy.

---

[109] Mary O'Leary.
[110] Son of James Burke and Mary O'Leary.

INDEX

A
Adrian IV, d. 1159, pope (1154-59), originally named Nicholas Breakspear, also known as Hadrian, 16.
B
bards, 55.
Barry, James (1761-1835), 20, 47, 52.
"Battle of Keimaneigh" (*poem*), 12, 14, 42-51, 56-7, 59.
Burke, James (1771-1847, husband of Mary O'Leary), 33-36, 143.
"By the River of Glenageary" (*poem*), 123-27.
C
Carrignacurra castle, 20-21, 24, 27-28, 38.
Carrignaneelagh castle, 18. 19. 20, 22, 24, 52.
Celts, 15-16.
Census of 1821, 30, 142-3.
Charles II, king of England (1660-85), 19, 24.
Corkery, Daniel, 55.
Cromwell, Oliver (1599-1658), 24-25.
D
"Dawning of the Day, The" (*poem*), 39, 57, 60, 67-69, 70-73.
Desmond, Earl of (Gerald FitzThomas), 19, 20.
Dromcarra castle, 21-22, 24.
E
Elizabeth I, queen of England (1558-1658), 23.
F
Famine, 29,30,36.
"Full Jug" (*poem*), 101-103.
G
George I, king of Great Britain (1714-27), 25.
George III, king of Great Britain (1760-1820), 38.
Gougane Barra, 18, 44, 52, 99 (footnote).
H
"Hard Plight" (*poem*), 59, 75-79.
Henry II, Norman king of England (1154-89), 16, 17.
Henry VIII, king of England (1509-47), 22, 40, 65.

Hoche, Gen. Lazare, 12, 38, 40, 63.
Hollow Sword Blade Corporation, 27.
"Hush, My Love" (*poem*), 39, 40, 81-83.

I

Inchigeelagh, 8, 12, 14, 15, 17-18, 20, 21, 24, 27, 30, 31, 34, 35, 36, 38, 43, 52, 133, 135, 137, 140, 141.

J

James VI and I, (*b.* 1566) king of Scotland (1567-1625), king of Great Britain(1603-25), 23.
James VII and II, (*b.* 1633, d. 1701) king of Great Britain (1685-8), 25, 27.

K

"Keening of John Burke, The" (*poem*), 34, 95-97.
Keimaneigh, battle of, 12, 14, 20, 34, 42-54.
Keimaneigh, Pass of, 8, 20, 21, 28, 29, 44, 45, 53.

L

"Lament for Art O'Leary" (*poem*), 13, 58, 128-32.
"Lament for John Burke" (*poem*), 34, 89-93.
"Lament for William Ring" (*poem*), 52, 98-99.
Lynch, Denis, 56, 105.

M

MacCarthy clan, 12, 14-15, 17, 18, 23, 25.
MacCarthy, Donogh (fourth earl of Clancarthy), 23-24, 25, 27.
MacMurrough, Dermot, 17.
Masters, Jasper, 38.
Munster, plantation of, 23-24.
Muskerry, barony of, 14, 15, 18, 19, 24.

N

Ní Chomhnaill, Eibhlín Dhubh (Dark-haired Eileen O'Connell) (widow of Munster folk hero Art O'Leary), 13, 53, 58, 128-132.
Ní Laoire, Máire Bhuí (*see O'Leary, Mary*)
Norman invasion, 16-17.

O

O'Connell, Daniel (1775-1847), 53, 128.
O'Donoghue, Fr. Denis, 7.
O'Laoire Bhuí (ancestral clan of Mary O'Leary), 21, 24.
O'Laoire, Art (founder of the Carrignaneelagh branch), 18-19.
O'Laoire, Capt. Keadagh, 25, 28.
O'Laoire, Conchobhar (father of Carrignaneelagh branch founder Art O'Laoire), 19, 23.

CPSIA information can be obtained at www.ICGtesting.com
Printed in the USA
BVOW03s2103080514

352825BV00001B/237/P